ROBINSON'S
WEIRD WORLD OF WONDERS
~~GREEKS~~ AND ROMANS

Sir Tony Robinson has been scribbling away since he was old enough to pick up a pencil. He's written long stuff (like a history of Australia), and shorter stuff (like this). He's rewritten old stories (like the ones about the Greek heroes Odysseus and Theseus), and made up new ones (for instance his children's TV series *Tales from Fat Tulip's Garden*). But history is what he likes best, because he says, 'How do you know who you are if you don't know where you came from?' That's why he's written Sir Tony Robinson's Weird World of Wonders, and he doesn't want to stop until he's written about every single bit of history there's ever been – although in order to do this he'll have to live till he's 8,374!

Del Thorpe has been drawing ever since that time he ruined his mum's best tablecloth with wax crayons. Most of his formative work can be found in the margins of his old school exercise books. His maths teacher described these misunderstood works as 'wasting time'. When he left normal school, Del went to art school and drew serious, grown-up things. Soon he decided the grown-up stuff was mostly boring, so went back to drawing silly cartoons and has done ever since.

Books by Sir Tony Robinson

Sir Tony Robinson's Weird World of Wonders series

British

Egyptians

Greeks

Pets

Romans

World War I

World War II

Bad Kids

The Worst Children's Jobs in History

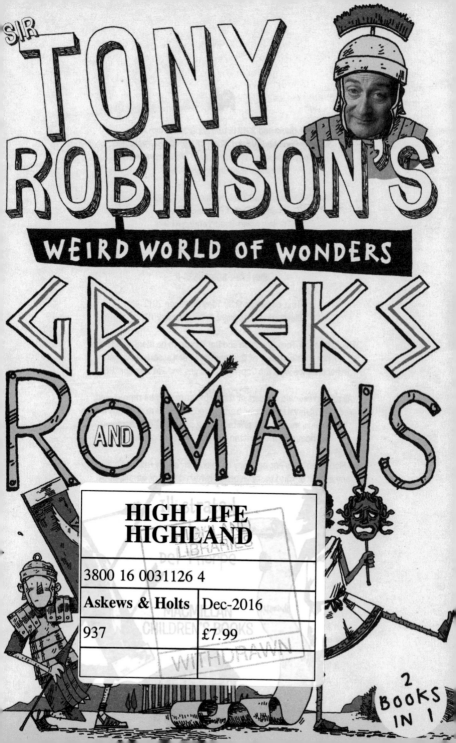

SIR TONY ROBINSON'S

WEIRD WORLD OF WONDERS

GREEKS AND ROMANS

2 BOOKS IN 1

First published 2012 in two separate volumes as
Sir Tony Robinson's Weird World of Wonders: Greeks and
Sir Tony Robinson's Weird World of Wonders: Romans
by Macmillan Children's Books

This edition published 2016 by Macmillan Children's Books
an imprint of Pan Macmillan
20 New Wharf Road, London N1 9RR
Associated companies throughout the world
www.panmacmillan.com

ISBN 978-1-5098-0539-6

Text copyright © Sir Tony Robinson 2012
Illustrations copyright © Del Thorpe 2012

The right of Sir Tony Robinson and Del Thorpe to be identified as the
author and illustrator of this work has been asserted by them
in accordance with the Copyright, Designs and Patents Act 1988.

1 3 5 7 9 8 6 4 2

A CIP catalogue record for this book is available from
the British Library.

Typeset by Dan Newman/Perfect Bound Ltd
Printed and bound by CPI Group (UK) Ltd, Croydon CR0 4YY

Jessica Cobb did the research for this book.
She's a bit like Jojo in the Curiosity Crew, although she's older,
cleverer and much bigger (Jojo's only 2cm* tall).
Apart from that they're identical, except that Jess has two heads
to store all her brains in. Thanks once again for all your hard work.

*Actually I'm nearly 3 cm tall!

The real Nits wishes to dedicate this book to **Louise Robinson**,
because Louise feeds her when she's hungry, takes her for walks,
cuddles her when they watch telly and tells her off when she gets silly.
Actually she does the same to me too, so I'll dedicate the book to Louise as well.

Hi! We're the Curiosity Crew. You'll spot us hanging around in this book checking stuff out.

It's about ancient Greece, a place full of myth and legend, olive oil and nude athletics.

It was also the birthplace of big brainboxes, mad scientists and war-crazy Spartans.

Read on to find out . . .

SWIMMING IN SOUP

Congratulations! You saved up your pocket money for five whole weeks and have now finally bought the book of your dreams – *Tony Robinson's Ancient Greeks*.

Am I right?

No?

OK. You wrote a long list of all the fabulous presents you wanted for your birthday and top of that list was this book.

Wrong again?

Did you find it in a wheelie bin?

Did it drop into your hands from a passing spacecraft?

Well, however you got hold of it – you're really, really curious to turn the page and find out what it's all about, aren't you?

Aren't you?

Go on, dive in!

Brilliant! You did it!

You've just followed in the footsteps of the ancient Greeks.

How?

Because just like you, the Greeks wanted to find out about things. They spent tons of time asking questions, arguing, poking stuff with sticks and testing things till they broke.

And by doing this, they came up with all sorts of inventions and discoveries – from an early computer to a laser death ray! (I'm not joking).

STIG'S BRILLIANT GREEKS NO. 1: THE GREEK WHO WAS BRILLIANT AT TELLING STORIES

Homer was a blind poet who told really exciting tales. His story about the war between the Greeks and the Trojans is probably the oldest to have been written down anywhere in Europe. There are older stories in other parts of the world, but most of them are pretty boring. The great thing about Homer is that all his characters seem so real, and they have such scary adventures. There is one in which the hero Odysseus (pronounced 'Odd-iss-yuss') has been trapped in a cave with all his sailors by a one-eyed giant, who starts eating them one at a time. Will Odysseus escape, or will he end up as a spoonful of mincemeat in the mouth of a foul-breathed giant . . . ?

You'll just have to read the story and find out, won't you!

The Greeks were among the first people in the world to use money, study history, work out complicated sums and write music.

Loads of things that we do today are because of the ancient Greeks.

FROGS ON A POND

OK! So you're probably wondering who these Greeks were.

Look at this map. ——————————

It's full of dots, isn't it? Lots of little islands and cities dotted around the Mediterranean Sea.

Ancient Greece wasn't really a country. It was a collection of island-states and city-states. Some of them were famous like Athens, Sparta, and Knossos, but there were lots of others too.

Each state was its own little country with its own way of doing things. They banded together in times of crisis but they also spent a lot of time squabbling with each other!

The main bit of Greece is very rocky and difficult to farm, so most Greeks lived on the coast or on islands, where they could make money from the sea by trading or fishing.

One Greek writer said the Greeks were like *'frogs sitting around a pond'.*

Which seems a pretty good description to me – that is, if frogs wore cute little tunics and were good at philosophy and maths.

So how did ancient Greece start?

Well, in order to answer that, we'll have to dive in a bit deeper.

GREEK SOUP

People started living in Greece more than 8,000 years ago, but annoyingly they didn't begin writing anything down for another 4,000 years.

So all we're left with from the earliest days of the Greeks are little bits of stories, legends and archaeology.

Get your cossie on.

Hurry up, girls!

Looking back into ancient Greek history is like peering into a big bowl of thick soup – bits of food float to the surface but you can't see the bottom of the bowl.

Imagine if you were swimming around in a bowl of Greek soup, with lots of ancient stories and bits of information bobbing up around you.

MYTH: Once upon a time a powerful king called Minos ruled the city-state of Knossos. In his huge palace was a giant maze, and at its heart lived a terrible monster.

FACT: In the rubble where Knossos once stood, archaeologists have found the remains of a gigantic palace that would have been home to a powerful Greek ruler around 1500 BC. It's got more than 13,000 interconnecting rooms, passages and staircases.

Sounds a bit maze-like to me! Maybe that's where the idea of the giant maze came from.

MYTH: One day the Prince of Athens went to a friend's wedding. A gang of creatures called centaurs who were half-man and half-horse burst in, drank all the wine and tried to kidnap the bride. But the prince drew his sword and defeated them.

Maybe this tale comes from the time when the Greeks first came into contact with horse-riding nomads. Imagine if you'd never seen one before. He'd look like a man and a horse glued together, wouldn't he?

So, sounds like these ancient cities really were rich.

MYTH: The son of the King of Troy stole the wife of the King of Sparta. The Spartan king was very angry and asked his brother, the mighty King of Mycenae, to help him get his wife back.

FACT: In the nineteenth century some incredible golden masks were found buried on a hillside in Mycenae. They were more than 3,000 years old.

MYTH: The Greeks launched a thousand ships which sailed to Troy and laid siege to it. The two armies fought for ten long years before Troy was finally burned to the ground, and the Greeks took back their queen.

Troy – where's Troy?

FACT: We're pretty sure it's in Turkey. The remains of a city have been discovered that was inhabited for thousands of years. It was destroyed several times, and fits the description of the legendary city.

Maybe bits of this story are true. But we'll probably never know for sure about the details.

Hmmm! So if Mycenae was real and Troy was real – does that mean the whole story's real?

11

THE FABULOUS CITY

What we know about very ancient Greece is as soupy as soupy can be.

But then around 3,000 years ago, the soup began to disappear.

Did a giant drink it? Did the bowl crack, so the soup leaked out on the table?

Don't be stupid! There wasn't really any soup.

It was around this time that the Greeks invented their own alphabet, started trading with lots of faraway countries, made loads of money, created their own heroes and began telling long adventure stories about them.

Families grew bigger, more people survived into old age, and soon there wasn't enough room for everyone. So Greek adventurers began doing the same thing as their heroes – sailing to foreign lands and setting up cities there.

It's just a way of saying that about 750 BC we start being able to understand what was happening in Greece more clearly.

So where did this piece of carrot come from?

But however far away from Greece they lived, there was one city back home they always remembered. It was a city so famous and so beautiful it made people proud to be Greek. And it was called ... **Athens!**

Once upon a time . . .

. . . in the long-ago days of myth and legend, the goddess Athena looked down from her home, Mount Olympus, on to the land below. Greece was a hot and rocky place. Its islands were bleached and barren, its mountains were high and it was starved of fresh water. All of it, that is, except for one small but beautiful triangle of green rolling hills surrounded by a dazzling blue sea – the land of Attica.

15

'This will be my land, and I will protect its people,' thought Athena, and floated down to Attica to tell everyone her plan.

But the gods of Greece were an argumentative bunch, and no sooner had she drawn breath than a vast waterspout rocketed out of the sea, and on its crest, riding a giant tuna fish, appeared her Uncle Poseidon, god of the oceans.

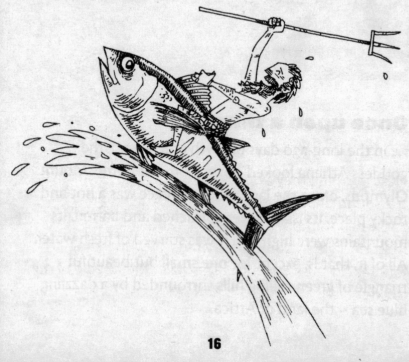

'Leave these people be!' he roared, 'for I will be their protector.'

But Athena wasn't having any of that. She stamped her foot, and an earthquake shook the land.

Poseidon seized the enormous waterspout in his mighty hands, bundled it into the shape of a storm cloud, hurled it into the air and drenched the Atticans in torrents of rain.

'Excuse me!' shouted a particularly brave young Attican (and he had to shout very loud so he could to be heard over the thunderous storm). 'Shouldn't we be allowed to choose who our protector will be?'

And as both gods seemed too surprised to reply, he added, 'Maybe if each of you gave us a really good present, it would help us decide.'

Excuse me!

'It would,' agreed the other Atticans furiously nodding their heads. 'It definitely would.'

Next morning they awoke to the sound of bubbling water, and when they opened their front doors they could see a brand-new sparkling fountain in the shape of a big tuna in the middle of the town square.

'This must be Poseidon's gift,' they said. 'How handy! Fresh water whenever we need it!' and they raced to the fountain with their cups and mugs and saucepans, and started to drink.

'Bleughhh!' they went. 'It's salt water! That's disgusting!'

'I'm going to be sick behind this little tree,' said the brave young Attican.

'What little tree?' demanded his sister. 'There's no tree here.'

BLA!

But she was wrong. There was now. It was Athena's present. It had olive-coloured leaves and olive-coloured berries, and was in fact an olive tree.

'Olive oil!' exclaimed the brave Attican, quite forgetting how sick he'd been feeling. 'That's what we'll make from now on. We'll rub it on our bodies to keep our skin smooth, we'll cook with it to stop our onions from burning, we'll make perfume with it so our armpits don't smell, and we'll burn it in our lamps so we can see at night. What an amazing present!'

'Thank you, Athena!' shouted the Atticans. 'In return we'll call our town Athens, and we shall be known as the Athenians.'

Up on Mount Olympus Athena smiled. From now on she'd make sure Athens was the most powerful, happening city the Greeks had ever seen.

LOVELY OLIVE OIL

The Athenians loved olive oil. They even gave it as prizes in their athletic games. Winners of chariot races took home 5 tons of olive oil – that's more than ten thousand bottles!

THE GROWTH OF ATHENS

Athens was built round a steep, rocky outcrop called the Acropolis.

Back in the days when the Greeks first started living in the area, they'd lived next to this big hill, so that if any enemies approached they could escape up to the top of it and throw stones down on them.

Then the early kings of Athens built a palace fortress on the Acropolis, and from it they ruled the rest of Attica.

But by the eighth century BC there was no longer any need for a palace – because Athens no longer had a king . . .

Normally in the Ancient World you were ruled by a king or a queen who made all the decisions and nobody argued with them. If you didn't have a big shiny crown on your head you had to shut up and do what you were told.

But the Athenian noblemen got fed up with having a king telling them what to do all the time, and decided to try something else instead.

First they became an '**aristocracy**'. The richest, poshest people in Athens, the aristocrats, took over running the city.

'Aristocrats' comes from the word 'aristoi' meaning 'best people' – because they thought they were better than everyone else.

But this was only slightly better than having a king – instead of one rich upper-class loudmouth being in charge, now there were several!

Then they tried being a **'tyranny'**. A series of rulers called 'tyrants' came along. They offered to kick out the aristocrats and do lots of nice things for the poor people of Athens if they helped the tyrants to seize power. At first this seemed like a good deal. Unfortunately, not all the tyrants kept their promises. A lot of them were really mean! And once they were in power, it was difficult to get them out!

Tyrant comes from 'tyrannos', meaning an illegal or oppressive ruler – not much fun, then!

Finally a politician called Cleisthenes (pronounced 'Klice-thin-knees') came up with a brilliant idea. He told the Athenian men that if they joined up with him and fought off the latest tyrant, he'd give them a say in how the city was run.

Oi, put some clothes on!

23

And sure enough the Athenians won the battle, kicked out the tyrant, and Cleisthenes' new way of running things was put into place. The Greeks had to make up a new word for this new system, and they called it '**democracy**' meaning 'government of the people'.

STIG'S BRILLIANT GREEKS NO. 2: THE GREEK WHO WAS BRILLIANT AT DIFFICULT SUMS

Pythagoras said there was no such thing as the perfect sausage. He thought every sausage in the world was slightly different, and every one of them was slightly wonky in some way or other. None of them was perfect, and the same was true of every chicken, every cup, every spider and every hat. In fact the only things that were perfect and always stayed the same were numbers. The number 6 for instance was never 5 or 6 ½, it was always plain old 6. He reckoned this made numbers the most important thing in the universe, and were the secret behind everything else. In fact he got so excited about numbers that he invented sums that are still used by scientists today, two and a half thousand years later. His followers thought he was pretty cool; they even set up a secret society to practise what he taught them.

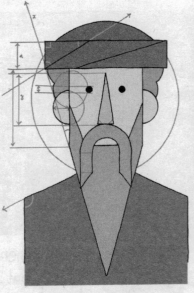

But he also believed that when humans died, they were born again as animals, and once when he heard a dog barking, he thought it was the sound of his dead friend – maybe he needed to get out more!

WHAT A BIG LADY!

The first temples on the Acropolis were little plain ones, but as Athens grew richer, wealthy people paid for them to be rebuilt bigger and better.

Until in 450 BC, the Athenians dragged more than 20,000 tons of gleaming white marble up to the top of the hill and built their biggest and best temple yet. They called it the 'Parthenon'.

No expense was spared: it would have cost you one silver talent to buy a massive warship – the Parthenon cost 469 talents!

It's still there in Athens, but it's been knocked about a bit.

The roof was held up by 48 giant columns. It was decorated by the best artists in Greece and inside was a 40-foot statue of the goddess Athena . . . Just imagine how freaky it would be to stand in front of a statue the size of a four-storey building!

What's more, the statue was covered in gold – another 44 talents' worth!

The Parthenon is ancient Greece's most famous monument and it's still standing in Athens today – although some bits have gone missing (including all the gold), and the statue isn't there any more . . .

LOSING YOUR MARBLES

In the 1800s, a British aristocrat called Lord Elgin was in Athens and, being a bit of a fan of ancient Greece, he went to take a look at the Parthenon. He liked it so much that he wanted to take a bit home with him. So he did (back then you didn't argue with a Lord). In fact he took more than a bit – he hired a team of blokes to dismantle massive chunks of the marble temple and ship them back to Britain.

When people suggested that this might be stealing, he said that the Greeks hadn't been looking after it properly and that really he was doing everyone a favour by 'rescuing' some of it . . . so that was all right then.

Elgin sold the bits he'd taken to the British Museum. They're now called the 'Elgin Marbles', and you can go and see them if you're in London. Lots of people are very cross about all this and the Greek government has spent years trying to get them back! In fact they've got a beautiful empty glass room in the New Acropolis Museum of Athens, just waiting for all the bits to be returned.

PICNICS ON THE PNYX

Not far from the Acropolis was a smaller hill called the Pnyx, and it had a large open-air theatre cut into its top.

The word 'Pnyx' means 'crowded', because every few weeks thousands of Athenians would make their way up the hill at dawn, carrying picnics and comfy cushions. They'd all squeeze through the narrow entrance, past the guards on the gate and into the theatre. When it was full, red security ropes were pulled across the street up to the hill to stop any more people getting through.

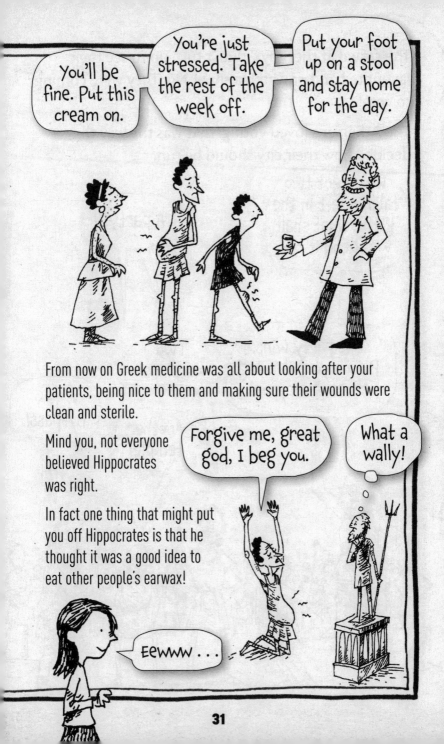

You'll be fine. Put this cream on.

You're just stressed. Take the rest of the week off.

Put your foot up on a stool and stay home for the day.

From now on Greek medicine was all about looking after your patients, being nice to them and making sure their wounds were clean and sterile.

Mind you, not everyone believed Hippocrates was right.

In fact one thing that might put you off Hippocrates is that he thought it was a good idea to eat other people's earwax!

Forgive me, great god, I beg you.

What a wally!

Eewww . . .

The crowd at the 'Pnyx' didn't turn up to see their favourite band or watch a show. No. They were coming to vote!

The Athenians loved voting; that was the way they decided how their city should be run.

Not everybody could take part – slaves, women, foreigners and children didn't get a vote.

But that still left at least 30,000 people!

Of course not all 30,000 turned up every time there was a vote. Lots of them had work to do, lived too far away or simply couldn't be bothered.

Usually only about six thousand attended . . . but that's still a massive amount of people.

HOW TO GET RID OF AN ANNOYING PERSON

When anyone became too powerful or irritating, the Athenians had a special system for getting rid of them. They wrote the name of the person on broken pieces of pottery called 'ostraka' (the ancient Greeks used these instead of scraps of paper, because in those days paper was really expensive and came all the way from Egypt), and put them in an urn.

If the annoying person got more than six thousand votes they had to leave the city for ten years. If they came back before their time was up, they were executed.

Is there anyone you'd like to get rid of like that?

THE DREADFUL IRON COLLAR

If you committed a serious crime in Ancient Athens you went before a jury – just like today except instead of twelve people, Athenian juries had *five hundred* people on them! They'd listen to the speeches made by the defendant and the accuser, then they'd vote by dropping metal discs in one of two jars, depending on whether they thought the person was innocent or guilty.

WHAT TIME IS IT?

Speeches were often timed to
make sure everyone got an equal
say. The Greeks did this using
clocks made of water! I know
water and clocks don't normally
go together; if you pour water
into a clock, it'll stop!

But the Greeks didn't use the
type of clocks we have today.
They took a small clay pot and
put a little hole in the base. Then
they filled it with water. As the
water leaked out, the level went down and
revealed lines drawn on the inside of the pot, which told
you how much time had gone by. Clever, eh?

If you were found guilty you could face exile or death.
Exile meant you were banished from the city. The
Athenians thought Athens was so great that having to
live anywhere else was a truly terrible punishment!

But not as terrible as being forced to drink poison or
being fastened to a big board by an iron collar round
your neck, and having the collar slowly tightened until
you were strangled to death. These were both common
forms of execution and compared with them, exile
probably didn't seem so bad.

HOW TO MAKE A NAME FOR YOURSELF

CRIME	PUNISHMENT
Lazing about too much	DEATH!
Looking weird	DEATH!
Yawning three times	DEATH!
Ignoring a cat	DEATH!
Murder	DEATH!
Stealing a cabbage	DEATH!
Stealing a sprout	DEATH!
Pretty much anything	DEATH!

In 621 BC before democracy was invented, a ruler of Athens called Draco had a clever idea. He decided to write down all the laws and put them up where everybody could see them. That way everyone would know what the law was.

Unfortunately, once he'd written them out, people started to wish he hadn't. Draco's laws were really harsh. The punishment for stealing a cabbage was death. The punishment for 'idleness' was death. In fact the punishment for nearly everything was death.

Even today, thousands of years later, really severe laws are still called draconian . . . well that's one way to make yourself famous!

DIFFERENT PLANETS

Boys and girls in ancient Greece might as well have lived on different planets!

Even as babies they were treated differently. Baby boys were treasured possessions, while baby girls were often chucked out on the street at birth.

Oh waah! I'm a girl!

Greek parents had the right to get rid of any kids they didn't want. If a baby was sick or unwanted, it was taken somewhere far away and ditched. Sometimes a nice rich childless couple would come along, find the baby and adopt it . . . but most times they didn't.

Greek parents nearly always wanted a boy – because a boy would probably grow up to be strong and rich and look after his parents when they were old and doddery. Girls, on the other hand, weren't allowed to earn money, and were likely to get married and look after somebody else's doddery parents. So their parents didn't think they'd be much use to them!

Even if your mum and dad chose to keep you and not chuck you out, life didn't get much better for girls . . .

STUCK AT HOME

Girls in Greece spent most of their life stuck at home. They weren't even allowed to go shopping! Just imagine if you'd been an ancient Greek girl – what would you have done on Saturdays?

So while Greek men spent lots of time outdoors going to work, hanging out with their mates, buying stuff and generally running the place, women did the cooking, cleaning and sewing . . . No wonder Pandora opened the box. At least it was something exciting to do!

OPEN THE BOX!

Ancient Greek men believed women were trouble with a capital 'T'! And they thought it had all started with the very first woman in the world – Pandora.

They said that Zeus – the king of the gods – gave Pandora a box and told her not to open it under any circumstances.

(Which if you ask me was a daft thing to do – everyone knows that when you give somebody a box and tell them not to open it, the first thing they do is try and open it . . .)

So Pandora tiptoed over to the box, looked around to make sure no one was watching her, then very, very carefully opened the box just a tiny bit, and . . .

BOOOM!!

Every single evil thing – Disease, Crime, Hatred, Envy and all the rest – escaped from it into the world. Terrified, Pandora slammed down the lid, but it was too late – all the evils had been released. The only thing left in the bottom of the box was Hope.

After that, the men decided it would be safer to keep women at home under lock and key, where they couldn't cause any trouble. Although personally I think it was just an excuse so they could go down the pub with their mates. I mean, think about it! Who was the troublesome person in the story – Pandora who opened the box, or Zeus who put all the evils of the world in a box but didn't lock it?

BURGLARY MADE EASY

The ancient Greeks built their houses out of mud bricks. Mud houses are good because they're cheap to make, but they're bad because their walls are so weak. In fact Greek burglars were called 'wall diggers' because they used to dig through the walls of houses to get inside and nick all the stuff!

But if you managed to keep the burglars away, you could live a very nice life in an ancient brick house. The rooms weren't built on top of one another . They were set out around a central courtyard. Greece was a hot

country even back then, so most families preferred to chill out in the courtyard rather than inside – a bit like having an outdoor living room.

Around the courtyard were lots of different sorts of rooms – kitchens, storerooms and bedrooms. At the front of the house was a dining room, where the head of the family (a man) asked his mates (other men) round for dinner parties. They'd all lie on couches, munch food, talk politics, read poetry, listen to music and get drunk.

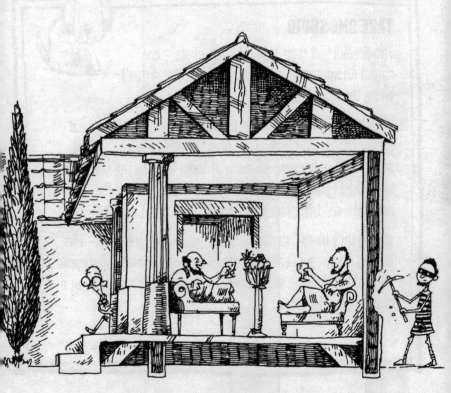

Hmm, that looks a bit fishy to me!

TAKE ONE SQUID

The Greeks had their own celebrity chefs – one called Archestratus (pronounced 'Ark-est-rah-tus') – wrote the first ever cookery book!

Most of this book was about fish. The ancient Greeks did eat bread, beans, fruit and olives, plus the odd kebab or a bit of sausage. But, because so many of them lived by the sea, what they liked eating most of all was fish – and not just fish with fins and tails and little faces, but all types of weird seafood.

In fact they liked fish so much they gave it as presents – the picture on one ancient vase shows a boy bringing his girlfriend an octopus! (Maybe she'd have preferred a bunch of roses or a big box of chocolates . . .)

At Greek dinner parties, men ate with their fingers (knives and forks hadn't been invented yet) and played drinking games like 'kottabos', which involved the diners flicking wine from their glasses and trying to hit a target.

If your mum's Greek and you try this at home and get a bullseye, she'll probably pat you on the head and tell you what a clever darling you are.

If your mum isn't Greek and you try it, she'll probably stop your pocket money for a week and send you to bed without any tea.

Oi! Pack it in!

That's a
Greek urn.

TOTALLY POTTY

With so much food, wine and olive oil around, the ancient Greeks had to find something to put it all in. Clay pots, jugs, cups and vases were the ancient Greek version of our plastic packaging.

Thousands of pieces of Greek pottery survive. The Greeks liked painting pretty pictures on their pots – stories of gods and monsters or scenes of daily life – so they can tell us a lot about ancient Greece.

Today some people pay millions of pounds for a Greek vase! Maybe that's what your old lunchbox will be worth in two thousands years' time!

What's a Greek urn?

Not a lot, they're all skint!

That's joke's even older than me!

Women weren't invited to these parties – in fact whenever men came round, all the women and girls were sent to a room at the back of the house and were expected to keep themselves busy doing girly things like sewing dresses, brushing each other's hair, and stroking kittens . . . and whatever else it is girls do!

GREEK FASHIONISTAS

In fact what women spent most of their time doing was making everyone's clothes (there wasn't a Primark in ancient Greece). This wasn't too difficult as both men and women wore simple loose tunics, pinned up and with a belt around the waist.

You could always jazz your outfit up with a bit of jewellery – women had their ears pierced and wore earrings as well as bracelets, necklaces and anklets.

Greek men often wore a ring with a design on it that could be stamped into clay or wax to seal documents.

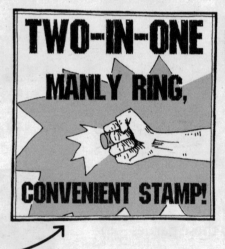

TWO-IN-ONE MANLY RING, CONVENIENT STAMP!

Having a golden tan was really fashionable if you were a man, but women tried to look as pasty as possible and painted their faces with chalk or white lead to lighten their skin.

*Because...
ladies love lead*

LEAD

HOW TO BE A GOOD BOY . . . IN THE NUDE

Probably the only good thing about being a girl in ancient Greece was that you didn't have to go to school. From the age of six, most boys were sent there to be taught important skills.

Peewee's List of . . . THINGS GREEK BOYS WERE TAUGHT IN SCHOOL

1 **Really really *really* long poems –** All Greek boys were expected to know the works of Homer (no, not Simpson – the original Homer we told you about on page 5). His most popular poem was about the war between the Greeks and the Trojans. It's over 15,000 lines long and would have taken about 24 hours to recite from start to finish (without a loo break) . . . Now that's what I call a long poem. That might seem impossible to learn, but it's full of people being killed in battles – and there's nothing like blood-spurting, spine-ripping, eye-popping violence to get boys learning poetry.

2 **Naked PE** – Greek boys had to be strong and athletic, because they'd probably become soldiers when they were older. They went to gyms, where they were taught wrestling, running, jumping, discus and javelin throwing. But they couldn't get out of it by saying they'd forgotten their gym kit, because they had to do their exercises naked! Imagine having to strip off every time you did PE!

Erm . . . let's see what's happening over here . . .

What? I'm not bothered.

3 **How to play a lyre** – The Greeks loved music, and most boys were expected to be able to bash out a tune on a lyre – an instrument that was a bit like a little guitar made of a tortoise shell with strings of twisted sheep gut. If you could sing a bit too, that was even better. We don't know what Greek music  sounded like, but a bunch of school boys twanging animal guts doesn't sound great to me.

If running around naked, reading poetry and playing instruments didn't appeal to you – well, tough. Greek parents employed a slave called a 'paidagogos' (which means 'child leader' in Greek) who took you to school and made sure you paid attention!

SLAVING AWAY

How many times have you wished you had a slave to do everything for you? . . . Well, you'd have loved living in ancient Greece.

Most families had one or two slaves to help around the house. Today we've got machines to help us, back then they had slave-operated devices . . . Instead of a vacuum cleaner you had a slave with a broom, instead of a dishwasher you had a slave with a sponge, instead of a microwave you had a slave with a cooking pot, and instead of a TV you had a slave in a box in the corner of the sitting room pulling funny faces . . . (OK, I made that last one up.)

Some Greeks sold their children into slavery for money (guess which children they were more likely to sell? Correct . . . The girls). But often slaves came from outside Greece – the Greeks would win a war and capture the defeated enemy along with their wives and children.

Sometimes slaves were treated quite well – they'd get decent food, a bed and took part in family occasions. But don't be fooled; it wasn't a total jolly. They couldn't go out, get married or have children without their master's permission and they were whacked if they misbehaved.

Slaves also did other jobs; some were teachers and shopkeepers, others worked in factories, farms, and on board ships.

Most slaves had to work unbelievably hard, all day and into the night, seven days a week. But the ones who got the very worst deal were those who worked in Athens's silver mines. 30,000 of them slaved away underground getting silver out of the rock, dragging it up to the surface and washing it. Not only was it back-breaking work but the silver was mixed with lead – which is toxic – so any slave who worked there long enough died of lead-poisoning. Which really sucked.

While their brothers went to school, girls were taught how to cook and clean. Parents were so keen to get their daughters off their hands that they'd often picked out a future husband for them by the time they were six years old.

At fourteen, girls got married and went to live with their husband's family! Still at least it was a chance to leave the house . . .

Except once she was married, the only job a Greek girl had was to start popping out (boy) babies as soon as possible.

STIG'S BRILLIANT GREEKS NO. 4: THE GREEK WHO WAS BRILLIANT AT THINKING

Thinking's easy, isn't it? We all do it – even really stupid people. But how do you actually think? How do all those thoughts come into your head? How do you know everything isn't a dream? What does 'happy' mean?

Most people hadn't given this sort of thing a moment's thought until Socrates (pronounced 'Sock-rat-ees') and his mates came along. He was a short ugly-looking man who was always criticizing the rich nobles, but the rest of the Athenians liked him and made him a judge. Eventually though, in order to shut him up, he was put in prison and found guilty of messing with the minds of the young people of Athens. He was sentenced to death, given a cup of deadly poison, drank it and died.

No one remembers the Athenian nobles any more, but the thoughts of Socrates are still with us today.

THAT'LL BE TWO AND A HALF GOATS PLEASE . . .

The silver mined by slaves was used to make coins. In fact the Greeks were among the very first people ever to have money.

And if you're thinking 'So what?' then you've never thought about how useful money is . . . and not just for buying chips on the way home.

Ever wondered what people did before they had coins?

Answer: They used goats. Well, not just goats . . . they used all sorts of things – they traded animals or crops for other things they needed (like metal tools or a nice kebab). But let's use goats as an example.

There were lots of advantages to using coins rather than goats:

- Goats are difficult to carry around in your pocket.

- Not everyone wants a goat.

- Goats don't have their value written on them – so it's difficult to agree what one goat is worth.

- The average lifespan of a goat's 15 years. After that you need a new goat.

So coins were invented instead. And pretty soon the Greeks realized that they were useful for another reason as well. They already stamped a picture on their coins to show where

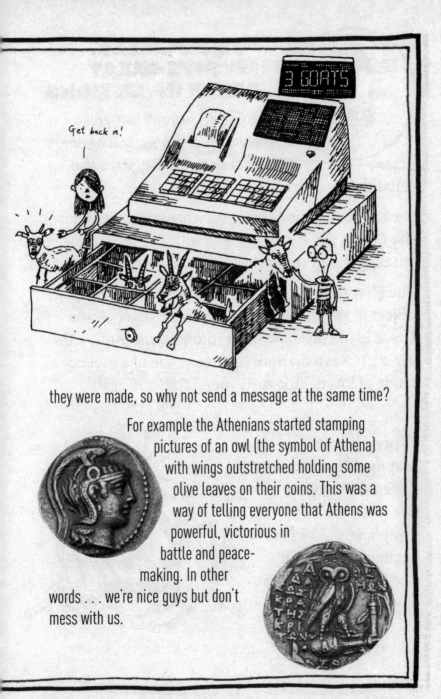

they were made, so why not send a message at the same time?

For example the Athenians started stamping pictures of an owl (the symbol of Athena) with wings outstretched holding some olive leaves on their coins. This was a way of telling everyone that Athens was powerful, victorious in battle and peace-making. In other words . . . we're nice guys but don't mess with us.

Jojo's List of ...
FIVE GREAT
GREEK INVENTIONS

The Greeks weren't just great at making up stories, and having brilliant thoughts. They were also seriously good inventors.

Next time somebody asks you what's so great about the Greeks you can wow them with this top five list of amazing things the geeky Greeks invented ...

The First Computer – In 1900, divers found a strange object in an ancient shipwreck under water off the Greek island of Antikythera (pronounced 'Ant-i-kith-ear-a'). It was a machine about the size of a shoebox made of lots of little rusty metal cogs and gears.

Experts think it was made by the Greeks to calculate the movement of the planets. Which technically makes it the first computer ever invented!

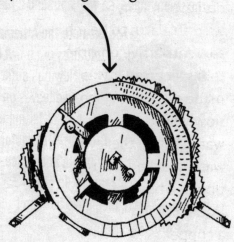

Catapults – Catapults are weapons that fire missiles (arrows, stones or even sometimes cows) at an enemy a long way away. The word comes from the Greek meaning 'shield piercer'. The Greeks designed massive powerful catapults – some of which were wound up and then released two missiles at once!

The Alarm Clock – Around 250 BC, the teacher Plato designed a water-clock with an alarm to help his students arrive on time to his lectures! It was made of a pot, which slowly filled up with water. When the level of water reached the top, it tipped a bowl of lead balls on to a copper plate and made a ringing sound!

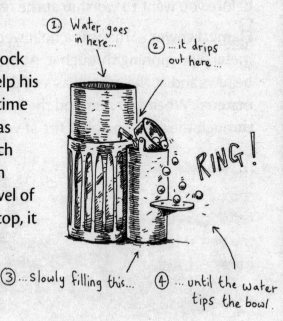

① Water goes in here...

② ...it drips out here...

RING!

③ ...slowly filling this...

④ ...until the water tips the bowl.

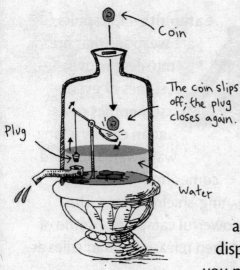

Coin

The coin slips off; the plug closes again.

Plug

Water

The Vending Machine – Next time you're getting a packet of crisps or a can of Coke out of a vending machine, just thank the Greeks! The Greek inventor Heron of Alexandria designed a machine that would dispense holy water when you put a coin in a slot. But it wasn't for drinking, it was for washing your hands before you went to worship at the temple!

Flamethrower – This was a hollowed-out log, with a metal pipe running through it. At one end was some bellows and at the other was a cauldron full of flaming material. When you pumped the bellows, the air shot through the tube and blew fire at your enemy!

PSYCHOPATHS

Stand by to meet the craziest bunch of psychopaths ever to call themselves Greek.

Basically take everything you've read about Athens and forget it. Unlike Athens, there was another city that didn't produce great thinkers, politicians and artists. The people of this city thought that swanky buildings like the Parthenon were a big fat waste of money and that thinking great thoughts was for losers.

Grrrrrr!

Their city was called Sparta, they were the Spartans and what they believed in was WAR and BATTLES and BLOOD.

THE SIEGE OF TROY

One thing the Spartans did share with the Athenians and the other Greeks was their love of the story of the Trojan War – because (a) it was a story about a war and the Spartans loved war, and (b) it was a story that featured . . . da da dahhh . . . yes, the Spartans. The whole Trojan War had supposedly kicked off because Helen, the beautiful wife of the King of Sparta, ran off with the son of the King of Troy.

The King of Sparta, Menelaus (pronounced 'Men-eh-lay-us') joined up with all the other kings of Greece and launched an attack on the city of Troy. The siege of Troy went on for ten long years until the Greeks came up with a clever plan.

They pretended to sail away, leaving a giant wooden horse on wheels as a gift for the Trojans (don't ask me why a big wooden horse is a suitable gift . . . nobody ever explains things like that in stories). But hiding inside the horse were thirty Greek soldiers.

The plan went perfectly – the Greeks pretended to leave and the Trojans opened the gates, saw the horse, thought it was the most terrific present they'd ever seen and pulled it inside the city. Then in the middle of the night, the soldiers crept out of the horse and opened the gate to the Greek army, who burned Troy to the ground, killed lots of Trojans and took the rest away as slaves.

Lessons from the story of Troy:

Don't mess with the Greeks.

Laying siege to a city takes a *long* time.

If someone ever leaves a giant wooden horse on your doorstep, call the police.

The Spartans were so proud of their role in the Trojan War (and the fact their king started it) that in 500 BC they built a shrine to King Menelaus and his wife Helen.

Spartan women visited the shrine to pray they'd be as beautiful as Helen. Spartan men went to pray that they'd be brave and mighty warriors like Menelaus.

Right, got me hat . . . Don't think I need anything else . . .

All Spartan men wanted to be brave – that's what being a Spartan was all about. They trained themselves up to be the most disciplined, awe-inspiring, unbeatable, make-your-enemy-wet themselves-and-run-away soldiers the world had ever seen.

And that meant that the whole of Sparta became one big military training camp . . .

Anything that got in the way of your training was banned – Spartan men didn't farm or fish, they didn't make things or trade with foreigners.

There was a small snag to this plan . . . it meant they didn't have any food. Hmmmm . . .

Well, luckily the Spartans had thought of this. They had people to do all the farming and fishing and making things for them! Slaves . . . lots and lots of slaves.

This wasn't the cushy type of slavery you got in Athens. This was proper slavery. Most people would rather have eaten a barrel of wasps than have been a slave in Ancient Sparta.

A HELL OF A LOT OF HELOTS

Where did they get all their slaves from?

Well, as the Spartans were pretty good at fighting (being as I think I mentioned the most disciplined, awe-inspiring, unbeatable, etc., etc., soldiers the world had ever seen), they went off and conquered a whole population of people living nearby and enslaved them.

These people were called the 'helots' (which meant 'captives') and they had to farm the land and do all the everyday jobs, so that Spartan citizens could carry on with their military training.

There were hundreds of thousands of helots in Ancient Sparta. In fact there were so many that they outnumbered Spartans by 10 to 1. This made the Spartans nervous – they were always worried about what would happen if the helots all got together and decided to revolt.

So helots were kept firmly under the thumb. In Ancient Sparta it was recommended that you beat your helots soundly at least once a year – even if they'd done nothing wrong – just so they knew who was boss!

There was even a special event each autumn when young Spartans were encouraged to go out at night and murder every helot they came across – which helped young Spartans get better at killing and kept helot numbers down at the same time!

WE'RE COMPLETELY SECRET

Maybe the Spartans weren't quite as weird and psychopathic as we believe. The trouble is they were really secretive, and hardly wrote anything down about themselves. So every story we know about them comes from people who didn't live in Sparta, or were the Spartans' bitter enemies . . . but I still wouldn't want to bump into one on a dark night!

The Big Book of Spartan Stories

CONTENTS

SHHHH!

SPARTAN LESSON 1: HOW TO KILL

As you've probably gathered by now, the Spartans had some odd ideas about the key skills a young boy needed . . . like the ability to sneak around at night and murder innocent people.

You might think you've got it tough – but that's only because you don't know what boys in Ancient Sparta had to go through.

First off, just as in Athens, any unwanted Spartan children were abandoned. Except that in Athens you might be left in a place where some kindly person could find you and adopt you . . . but in Sparta you were thrown over a cliff.

Dad's says he's taking me for a picnic . . . I've got a bad feeling about this . . .

There was a ravine a few miles outside Sparta called the 'place of rejection', and it wasn't a picnic spot! Babies who the Spartans thought were too sick or weak to be any use were taken there and chucked down it.

PLACE OF
REJECTION
No Picnics

STIG'S BRILLIANT GREEKS NO. 5: THE GREEK WHO WAS A BRILLIANT GENERAL

A few nights before Pericles (pronounced 'Perry-cleese') was born his mum dreamed she was about to give birth to a lion. Later his fans said this was a prophecy which foretold what a terrific fighter he'd become. But his enemies reckoned it just meant he was going to be a big-head!

Pericles became Sparta's greatest enemy, but his most famous victory wasn't really a victory at all. The mighty kingdom of Sparta decided to attack Athens. A lot of Athenians wanted to fight back, but not Pericles; he knew no one could beat the Spartan army. So he built enormous walls round Athens and told all the people of Attica to pack up their things and hide behind them.

Don't be frightened, I'm 'armless!

When the Spartans arrived they destroyed every little Attican town and village, but they couldn't get inside the big city. It was a terrible time for Athens, but Pericles was a brilliant talker as well as a brilliant fighter. He persuaded the Atticans not to surrender, and when the Spartan army finally gave up and went home, Pericles sent the Athenian navy out to smash the towns which had supported Sparta.

Exactly the same thing happened the following year, but this time it was even worse because a dreadful disease broke out in Athens and a lot of people died, including Pericles' two sons. But once again the Spartans left Athens without having conquered it, and Pericles' navy annihilated the Spartan allies.

Pericles was incredibly popular. He looked after the poorest Athenians; he even gave them free tickets to the shows in Athens's big theatre. He filled the city with magnificent buildings, some of which are still standing today over two thousand years later.

His enemies said he was arrogant, a swindler and not nearly as great as everyone else thought he was. But he won nine trophies for his skills as a general, and showed the whole world that, though Sparta might have had a superb army, the Athenians were smarter, and were determined not to be defeated by their arch-rival.

At seven years old, all Spartan boys were sent away from home to be turned into soldiers.

Most of their time was spent learning how to kill – but you'd also be taught a bit of reading (so you could read books about killing), maths (so you could count the numbers of people you'd killed) and music (to kill to).

To toughen them up, each boy was given only one piece of clothing to wear (a simple cloak ... dyed red to hide the spatters of blood you were bound to get all over it), and made to sleep rough outside even in winter.

Food was rationed, and boys were expected to steal to get extra food. But if you were caught you were severely beaten – although this wasn't to stop you stealing, it was to teach you to be a better thief!

A LITTLE NUTTER

One Spartan boy was so hungry he stole a fox and hid it under his shirt. Before he could kill it and eat it, he was made to stand in line for an inspection. Rather than get caught stealing, he stood there quietly while the fox clawed and chewed its way into his stomach, until he died. That was the Spartan way.

See, I told you the Spartans were nutters.

PIG'S BLOOD AND VINEGAR

To celebrate getting to the age of twelve without starving to death, freezing to death or having your insides eaten by a fox, Spartan boys got to take part in a special challenge.

Lots of delicious cheese was laid out on a table, but to reach the table you had to run past a lot of men attacking you with whips . . . I think I'd rather have had a nice party and some cake, wouldn't you?

But you didn't get cake in Sparta. Cake wasn't allowed. Cake was 'fun'.

The food in Sparta was notorious – the most common dish was called 'Black Broth', and it was made of pig's blood and vinegar. One visitor to Sparta joked that having tasted Spartan food, he could understand why they were all so willing to die!

Things weren't that much better when you became an adult. You weren't allowed to get married until you were thirty and you couldn't leave the army until you got to sixty!

DOUBLE TROUBLE

While other Greek cities got rid of their kings, the Spartans kept hold of theirs. In fact they didn't have just one king ... they had two! One to lead the Spartan army into battle, and the other to stay at home and look after Sparta.

Two kings meant two palaces, two royal families and twice as many arguments.

HERACLES

The Spartans believed they were descended from the Greek hero Heracles (or Hercules as some people call him). Heracles was the Superman of the Ancient World – half-human and half-god.

People said he was so strong that even as a baby he'd been able to take care of himself. Once, the goddess Hera (Athena's auntie) sent two snakes to kill him in his cot, but little Heracles just grabbed hold of them as if they were toys and strangled them with his baby fists!

When he grew up, Hera picked on him again – she drove him mad and he killed his own children in a frenzy. To earn forgiveness for this terrible crime he was made to carry out twelve really difficult jobs – these are called the 'Labours of Heracles'.

Among them he had to kill a whole bunch of monsters, including a big lion with arrow-proof fur (the 'Nemean Lion'), a nine-headed dragon called the Hydra, and a load of bizarre man-eating birds with metal feathers! He also had to steal loads of stuff – including a belt from the Queen of the Amazons and some golden apples from Zeus himself.

I love going clubbing!

With all that killing and stealing I'm not sure Heracles would make such a great role-model these days, but no wonder the nutty Spartans loved him!

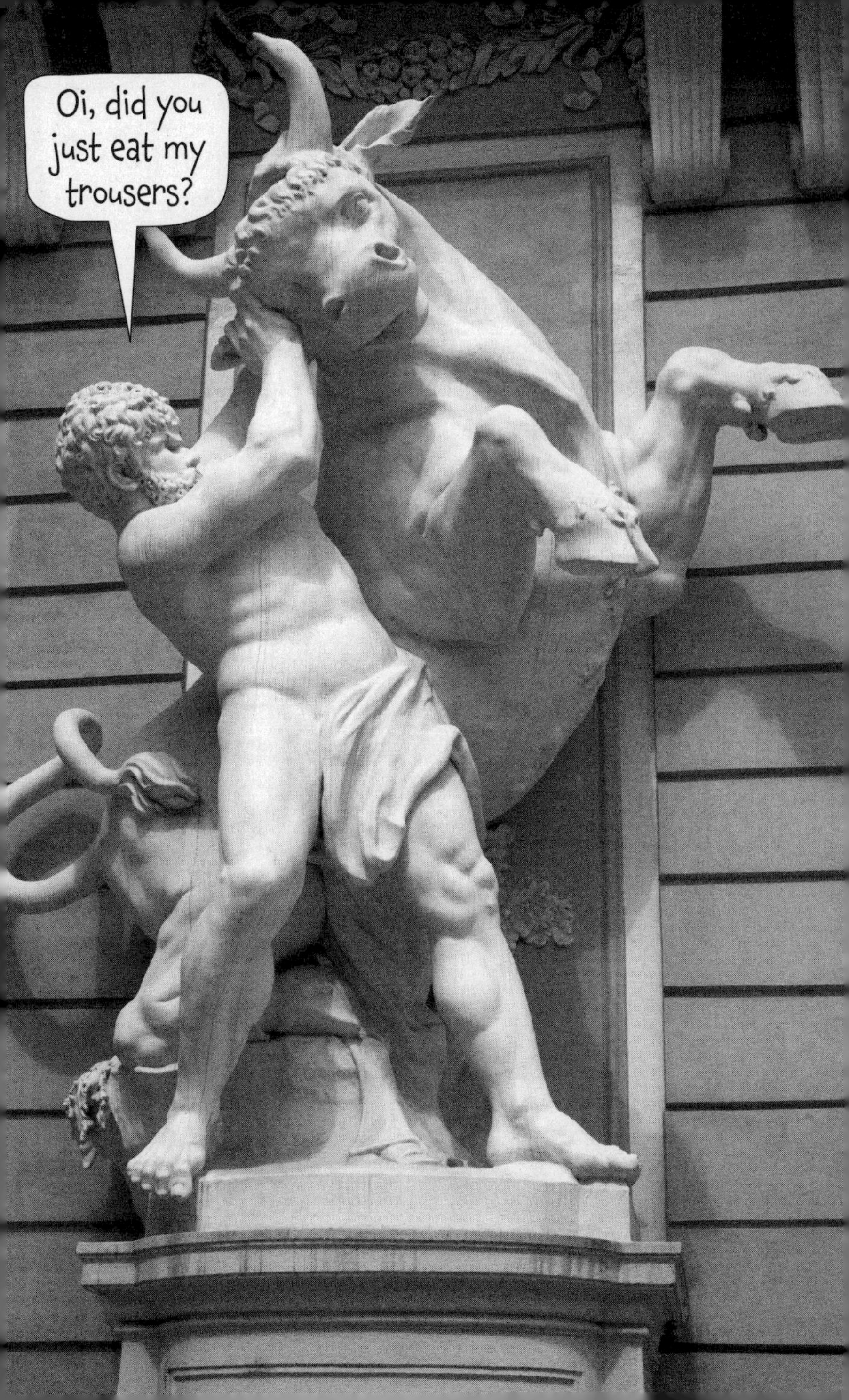
Oi, did you just eat my trousers?

SPARTAN GIRLS RULE

Being a girl in ancient Sparta was a world apart from a girl's life in other Greek cities. You got to leave the house for a start.

But more than that – just like boys – Spartan girls were taught to be strong and tough, and how to wrestle and throw javelins. They were also fed the same disgusting food and allowed to drink wine just like the boys.

Young Spartans by Edgar Degas.

Spartan women could choose who they married – what's more, they didn't usually get hitched until they were eighteen (which was pretty old for girls in ancient Greece). But as wives and mothers it was their duty to make sure their men didn't back away from a fight.

One Spartan wife said to her husband who was going off to war, 'Return carrying your shield or lying on it' – meaning either come back victorious or dead!

[sniff]
Why?

Spartan women were allowed to own their own property and were expected to be able to guard their homes against invaders while their husbands were away.

Yes, Spartan girls were really tough!

Greek men from other cities thought it was dreadful that Spartan women had so much freedom. But they probably didn't say so out loud when they were visiting Sparta – in case any Spartan women overheard them and punched them!

THE OLYMPIC GAMES

Athens, Sparta and the other Greek city-states never stopped fighting and squabbling. A bit like children, they argued about who was best and which city the gods loved most.

To find out, they held games.

I don't mean they spent wet weekends playing Scrabble.

I'm talking about big fancy competitions – music competitions, poetry competitions and athletics competitions . . . basically any opportunity to show off and get a prize at the end.

If you won you could say it was because the gods loved your city best, and all the losers in the neighbouring cities could go kiss your big hairy butt!

The most famous of all these games were the Olympic Games – maybe you might just have heard of them!

Today the Olympic Games are an international event involving athletes from all over the world – but back in ancient times, only Greeks took part. Every four years, the fittest and strongest athletes from all over the country came to compete and win glory for their hometown!

These games were held in honour of Zeus, king of the gods.

Hey, ladies . . . How you doing?

ZEUS

The Greeks had lots of gods, like Athena, Poseidon and Hera, but the mighty Zeus (pronounced 'Zoose') was ruler of them all.

His father Cronus had been told that eventually one of his children would overthrow him, and so to stop this happening, each time he and his wife had a baby, Cronus ate it up. Finally when his sixth child, Zeus, was born, his wife (who was fed up with all her children being gobbled up) wrapped a stone in a blanket and gave it to Cronus to swallow instead.

Zeus grew up, became king of the gods and rescued his brothers and sisters by forcing his dad to vomit them all up again!

Zeus had lots of wives and girlfriends. He would disguise himself as things like swans, white bulls, eagles, showers of gold and flames of fire in order to romance unsuspecting women!

The result of this was that he ended up as father to a whole host of kids including **Athena**, **Ares** the god of war, and **Aphrodite**, goddess of love.

Dad, stop chatting up women!

A WONDER-FUL STATUE...

The Olympic games were held at Olympia – a sacred place with a grand temple dedicated to the mighty Zeus.

Inside it was an enormous gold and ivory statue of Zeus sitting on a giant throne. As one visitor said, it looked as though if Zeus had stood up he'd have taken the roof off the temple!

This statue was so impressive it was known as one of the 'Seven Wonders of the World' (a list of the top seven sights all travellers should go and see).

Before the games started, the athletes would pray to Zeus that they would win their competition, and during the games 100 oxen were sacrificed as a way of thanking him for being such a marvellous god!

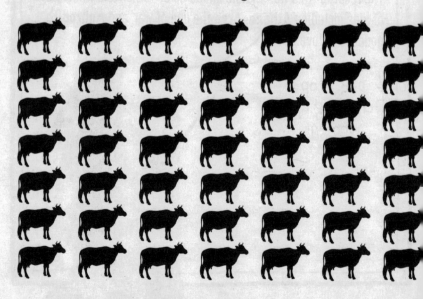

ON YOUR MARKS . . .

When the Olympics had first started there'd only been one event: a running race which was called the 'stadion' because the athletes had to run a single length of the stadium. Then more events were added because it hadn't been much fun for the spectators to travel for days to get to the games and then only see one short race.

So a there-and-back race was introduced and then a long-distance race. Over time more events were included like wrestling, boxing, long jump, relay races, chariot races, javelin and discus throwing.

Apparently we're all appearing in the opening ceremony.

Jojos Guide to . . .
THREE OF THE MOST DANGEROUS (AND EXHAUSTING) SPORTS IN THE ANCIENT OLYMPICS

Chariot Racing – This was the Formula 1 of the Ancient World. Chariots pulled by horses sped up and down a track, careering around a turning post at each end. These posts were known as the 'taraxippus' or 'horse-terror' because it was here that most crashes took place. Accidents were often fatal – the drivers either being crushed by the chariot or trampled by the horses.

Hoplite Race – 'Hoplites' was the name for Greek soldiers. Contestants in the Hoplite Race had to run a race in full armour complete with a big heavy shield and a helmet!

Pankration – A combination of boxing and wrestling. The word 'Pankration' (pronounced 'Pan-krat-ee-on') meant 'total combat' and there were only two rules – no eye-gouging and no biting. The two competitors kept fighting until one was knocked out, gave up or died!

The Panathenaic Stadium in Athens – site of the first modern Olympics in 1896.

The Olympics were a very big deal; over four days the best athletes in Greece came together to take part. This was sometimes tricky because the city-states were often busy fighting one another. So a two-month 'truce' was held while the games were on, allowing people to travel safely to Olympia and back without having to go through a war-zone.

But it wasn't just competitors and spectators who travelled to the games – fast-food sellers, souvenir sellers and gamblers who bet on the races turned up too! In fact it got so crowded that tents were put up for the Olympic village, more tents for the rich spectators and their servants, so the whole place was soon one massive campsite!

Women weren't allowed to take part or watch the events, because all the competitors were stark naked and it was thought that a lot of women gawping at them might put them off.

A mother once tried to get round this rule by turning up disguised as a male trainer. But she got so excited when her son won his race that she revealed her true identity. From then on the trainers had to be naked too – to stop any more women sneaking in!

If I win this, I'll be able to afford some pants!

SPORTS STARS
OF THE ANCIENT WORLD

The athletes who competed in the Olympics were the ancient equivalent of premiership footballers or basketball stars.

They trained hard for years before each event. And, just like sports stars today, they hired personal trainers to help them. Whole books were written with tips on how to train an award-winning athlete, full of the latest workouts and fad diets.

One former champion suggested a diet of nothing but dried figs. I'm not sure about winning races, but if you went on that diet you'd certainly run fast to the toilet!

An ancient Greek gym.
Looks a bit draughty.

BIG MILO

One famous wrestler, Milo of Croton, won SIX Olympic titles! He was supposed to have eaten 20lb of meat, 20lb of bread and drunk 18 pints of wine a day. That's the equivalent of munching your way through 40 massive burgers!

He once trained for the games by lifting a newborn calf and carrying it about on his shoulders every day. As it grew, so did his strength. Eventually it became a full-grown bull, which he continued carrying about until he got fed up with it, then he slaughtered it and roasted and ate it in one sitting!

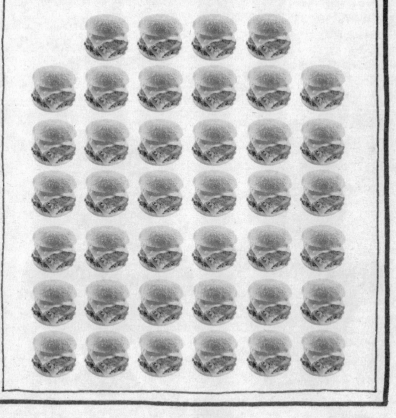

CHEATERS ALMOST NEVER PROSPER

When all else failed, some athletes resorted to cheating.

The first recorded incident was in 388 BC when a boxer called Eupolus of Thessaly bribed three of his opponents to take a dive, making it look as though he'd knocked them out.

At another games, one runner caught hold of his opponent's hair to slow him down so that he could sprint past him and win!

The officials did their best to put cheaters off – each competition had either a 'whip bearer' or a 'stick bearer' standing by to whack those who broke the rules.

Disgraced cheaters were also forced to pay hefty fines. Each fine paid for another statue of Zeus to be put up near the entrance of the stadium with the cheat's name on it in big letters– so that everybody would know what they'd done. Every athlete had to walk past these statues on their way to the games – how humiliating for the cheater!

I'm not sure they always give their real names . . .

na Sneak

Charlie Cheater

Tricky Ricky

CHAMPIONES!

If an athlete had trained hard enough (or cheated and managed not to get caught), they might be lucky enough to win. If they were hoping for a big shiny gold cup they'd have been disappointed – all they got was a crown of leaves and a red ribbon. The glory of winning was supposed to be prize enough.

But it was a different story when they got home. They were welcomed back like heroes, given a parade and awarded honours like free meals and a pension for life! Statues of them were put up and poems written about their incredible feats – they became celebrity sportsmen, famous throughout Greece!

DISCOBOLUS

Greek sculptors loved carving statues of athletes' perfect bodies.

One of the most famous ever made is of an Olympic athlete. We don't know his name – the statue is just called '**discobolus**' which means 'discus thrower' because, er . . . he's throwing a discus.

It's so lifelike that if you stood in front of it you'd be tempted to duck in case the discus took your head off. Which shows how good Greek sculptors were!

GREECE'S GOT TALENT!

You're through to the next round!

The Greeks didn't just hold competitions to see who was best at running, jumping and throwing things. They also held games that included music, poetry and acting competitions. The most popular of these were the Pythian Games at Delphi, held in honour of the god Apollo.

Just as the Olympic Games began as a single race, the Pythian Games had started off as one singing contest. The competitors had to see who was best at singing a hymn to Apollo, accompanied on a lyre. (See! – all those years at school twanging animal guts eventually paid off!)

Over time other musical and dance contests were included, and eventually acting and poetry reading. You can still see the remains of the huge outdoor theatre built at Delphi in the fourth century BC.

FART GAGS AND PANTOMIME HORSES

The Greeks invented theatre and everything that went with it – from the props and the scenery to the very first pantomime horse (one picture on a vase shows two men dressed up as a centaur)!

Every town had a theatre and thousands of people would turn up to watch performances. In Athens, even prisoners were sometimes temporarily released so they could go and see a play!

Actors (there were no actresses – this was ancient Greece, remember) wore masks with set expressions to show clearly what their character was thinking (big smiley face = happy; frown = angry, etc., etc.).

As the audience was sometimes a long way away from the stage (as many as 15,000 people turned up to watch some plays), the actors wore big padded costumes and platform shoes to make themselves

visible from a distance. A choir (called a 'chorus')
often stood beside the stage to sing about what was
happening – so that everyone could follow the story.

There were even special-effects machines. For instance,
there was a low platform on wheels which could be
pushed around the stage (often to wheel 'dead bodies'
on and off stage) and a crane that could make actors fly.

The two main types of Greek play were 'tragedies' and
'comedies'. The tragedies were sad and serious, the
comedies involved a lot of stupid fart gags, a lot of
making fun of the audience and a lot of filth! I wonder
which would be more popular today!

Jojo's List of ...
FIVE MORE GREAT GREEK INVENTIONS

The Alphabet – Did you know that the Greeks came up with lots of the letters we use today? The word 'Alphabet' even comes from the Greek for A and B (Alpha and Beta).

Αα	Ββ	Χχ	Δδ	Εε
Aa	Bb	Cc	Dd	Ee
Φφ	Γγ	Ηη	Ιι	Κκ
Ff	Gg	Hh	Ii	Kk
Λλ	Μμ	Νν	Οο	Ππ
Ll	Mm	Nn	Oo	Pp
Θθ	Ρρ	Σσ	Ττ	Υυ
Qq	Rr	Ss	Tt	Uu
Ωω	Ξξ	Ψψ	Ζζ	
Ww	Xx	Yy	Zz	

Automatic Doors – Heron of Alexandria designed temple doors which opened automatically. At the same time trumpets started to play, fog was pumped out and statues and metallic birds started singing . . . which must have completely freaked the worshippers out!!

Secret Codes – The Greek historian Polybius came up with a way of sending messages without writing them down. He invented a code which could be sent using fire beacons over long distances – each arrangement of torches signalled a different letter and nobody watching would know what you were saying!

Oi!

What?

Death Ray – The Greek mathematician Archimedes (pronounced 'Arky-mee-dees') was a bit mad. They say he was once sitting in the bath when he had a great idea and was so excited he jumped up and ran through the streets naked, shouting 'Eureka!' ('I've got it!'). One of his most bizarre inventions was the 'death ray' – a series of mirrors which concentrated sunlight on to enemy ships and set them on fire!

Showers – And last but not least, the Greeks loved having a good scrub at the public baths and were the first people with showers ... freezing cold ones!

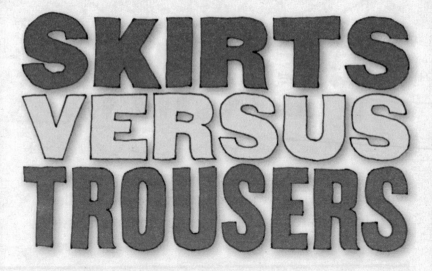

SKIRTS VERSUS TROUSERS

I n 500 BC everything seemed to be going great for the ancient Greeks.

Their cities were jam-packed with brilliant athletes, world-beating artists and writers, really clever philosophers, genius mathematicians and shrewd politicians.

There was a lot of money to be made, plenty of sun and loads of fish in the sea – Greece was the best place in the world! (OK, so the Spartans were a bit weird but they were good at track events and their army was first-class!)

Hardly anyone realized that a dark cloud was forming on the horizon. A mighty Empire was growing in the East, and it wanted to crush Greece like a bug. This Empire was called . . .

PERSIA!!

'The Persians' was the ancient name for the people who lived in what is today called Iran in the Middle East. They created one of the largest Empires in history, covering a massive 8 million square miles and three

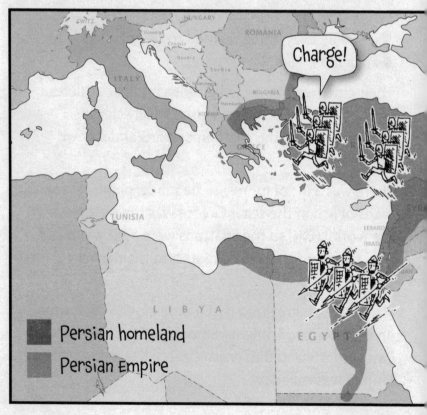

Persian homeland

Persian Empire

continents! The word 'Persia' actually *means* 'Empire'!

The Emperors of Persia ruled their kingdom with an iron fist – they used a network of roads and thousands of spies to keep an eye on every corner of their Empire. Gold and silver poured in from trade and taxes and was used to build spectacular monuments and an enormous, well-equipped army.

Were they scary?

Yes they were!

FASHION FORWARD

Did you know? The Persians invented trousers! The Greeks wore a simple tunic, a bit like a T-shirt and skirt sewn together. But the Persian fashion was for baggy trousers tucked into their boots, because it was more comfortable for horse-riding. The Greeks thought they looked ridiculous; as far as they were concerned, real men wore skirts!

As the Persian Empire expanded westwards, the Greeks started getting a bit nervous.

In 545 BC, the Spartans sent a warning to the Persian Emperor, Cyrus the Great. 'Stay away from Greece,' they said, 'or you'll have the Spartan army to deal with . . .'

When he received this message, Cyrus asked, 'Who are the Spartans?'

He'd never even heard of them!

Somebody kindly explained to him that Sparta was in Greece – a place full of brilliant athletes, world-beating artists and writers, genius mathematicians and so on and so forth . . . at which point, Cyrus immediately added Greece to his list of places to conquer.

If I wear this dressing gown, no one can laugh at my trousers.

Fortunately, Cyrus died before he could pop over there. But in 490 BC his successor, the Emperor Darius, sent an army to invade Attica. The Persian fleet landed a few miles from Athens, near the town of Marathon.

The Athenians had to stop them.

HOPLITES

Sparta was the only place in Greece with a full-time army, but every city expected its citizens to be able to fight when needed.

You bought your own armour and spear when you left school, and completed your basic training. From then on, whenever your city went into battle it called you up, and you had to get your kit out, dust it off and head out to defend your home city.

Greek soldiers were called 'hoplites', which means 'armoured' – because they were dressed head-to-toe in heavy bronze armour! This included:

a helmet

a breastplate

shin-guards

a large round shield covered in bronze called a 'hoplon'

Your shield was the most important bit of your kit. It not only protected you from blows but you could also use it to push forward into the enemy ranks. Hoplites would stand packed close together and overlap their shields forming a shield-wall. Then they'd poke their big spears over the top of their shields into the faces of the enemy.

All this kit was hot and heavy – Greek soldiers couldn't move very fast and they could probably only fight for about 30 minutes before passing out from exhaustion! But it also made them very difficult to kill – swords and arrows barely made a dent in all that armour.

The Persian army outnumbered the Athenians 2 to 1, but the Persians were only lightly armed with bows and arrows and wicker shields. Yes – *wicker* – the stuff people make waste-paper baskets out of . . . I know which side I'd rather have been on!

The two armies met near Marathon and the Athenians were victorious! One writer said that 6,400 Persians died and only 192 Athenians . . . although this could be an exaggeration – the Athenians were so excited at having won, they probably didn't spend a lot of time counting the bodies.

HOW DOES THE MODERN MARATHON GET ITS NAME?

When the Battle of Marathon had been won, the Athenians sent their fastest runner – a chap called Pheidippides (pronounced 'Fi-dip-e-deez') – to take the news of their victory back to Athens. After legging it 26 miles, the exhausted Pheidippides arrived home, gasped 'We've won' and then dropped down dead . . . Bet he wished the ancient Greeks had invented mobile phones.

Their defeat at Marathon put the Persians off invading Greece . . . but only for a little while.

THE INVASION OF THE CENTURY

It wasn't long before Darius's son Xerxes (pronounced 'Zurk-sees') was planning another invasion ... and this time it was going to be done properly. Xerxes mustered troops from all over the mighty Persian Empire – more than 250,000 soldiers from places as far away as Egypt, India and Africa.

He made sure *nothing* would get in his way – he ordered a bridge to be built over the channel separating Asia and Europe to carry his troops across, and a giant canal was dug to help his fleet of Persian ships reach Greece faster and more easily.

Xerxes was planning the invasion of the century! Everybody was talking about it. Especially the Greeks ...

Have you heard who's coming?

Those bossy Persians, I know ...

'WATER' LOAD OF RUBBISH

For a long time, people didn't believe that Xerxes really built a giant canal – no sign of it remained and experts didn't think it possible without mechanical diggers.

But using modern technology, scientists recently found evidence of the remains of it buried underground in northern Greece! Over a mile long and wide enough for two ships to pass, the canal must have been dug by hundreds of workers using just shovels and buckets on pulleys.

It allowed the Persian fleet to take a shortcut into the Aegean Sea. But after the invasion it must have silted up and become buried over time.

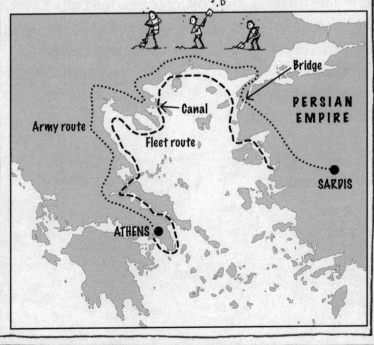

UNITED WE STAND

The Greek cities held a meeting and decided that the only chance they had of stopping the invasion was to join forces!

Either they stood together or Greece would become a province of the Persian Empire and they'd all have to start speaking Persian and wearing ridiculous trousers.

This time it wouldn't just be Athens doing the fighting: thirty-one Greek cities joined together under the leadership of Sparta.

THE THREE HUNDRED

As Xerxes' massive invasion force swarmed into Greece, the Spartan King Leonidas volunteered to lead a Greek army to defend the narrow pass of Thermopylae (pronounced 'Ther-mo-pih-lee') to prevent the Persians getting through. Among his forces were three hundred of Sparta's finest warriors.

The Persians were about to find out about the Spartans . . . the hard way.

Xerxes and his huge army finally arrived at Thermopylae and waited for the little band of Greeks in front of them to retreat . . . and they waited . . . and waited.

A Persian messenger delivered a warning: 'If you don't go away we will shoot so many arrows at you that it will blot out the sun!'

The Spartan replied: 'So much the better, we'll fight in the shade.'

STIG'S BRILLIANT GREEKS NO. 6: THE GREEK WHO WAS BRILLIANT AT WRITING PLAYS

Once upon a time there weren't such things as plays. There was only a bit of singing and dancing to keep the gods happy. Then people started coming to watch, so little stages were built to make it easier for them to see.

After that poems started being specially written for these little shows, and gradually the whole thing got more and more complicated until . . .

SHOWBIZ WAS BORN!

Ta-daah!

The very first proper play that still exists was written by a playwright called Aeschylus (pronounced 'Eeska-lus'). Before he became famous he'd been a soldier, and fought in the Battle of Marathon and the Battle of Salamis. So not surprisingly some of his plays were about the Persians.

In those days there were competitions all over Greece to find the most talented performers and writers, and Aeschylus nearly always won.

He died when he was hit by a tortoise which was dropped by a flying eagle . . . Honestly! And even though he had been such a celebrity, his gravestone doesn't mention his success in the theatre – it just says he fought bravely against the Persians.

Sorry for dropping in unannounced, mate!

The Emperor Xerxes was furious. He ordered his troops to advance and clear the pass – then sat back to watch the action.

What he saw was wave upon wave of Persians crashing against a wall of hoplites. No one had ever seen so many armed men held at bay by such a tiny fighting force. Xerxes threw everything he had against the Greeks but for two days the Persian bodies just kept piling up.

Finally on the third day Xerxes had a lucky break – a Greek traitor came to him and told him about a secret path around the pass.

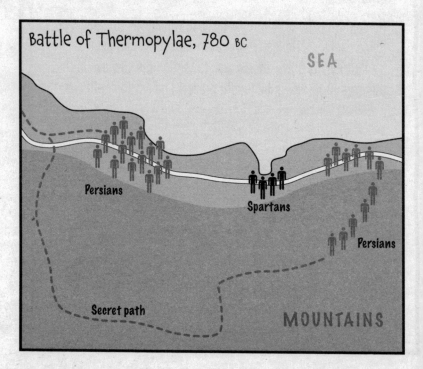

Battle of Thermopylae, 780 BC

SEA

Persians

Spartans

Persians

Secret path

MOUNTAINS

STIG'S BRILLIANT GREEKS NO. 7: THE GREEK WHO WAS BRILLIANT AT INVENTING HISTORY

The reason that we know so much about what happened in the Persian Wars was that a Greek called Herodotus wrote about it.

He grew up just after these wars had finished – everyone was talking about how surprising it was that Greece had won.

He decided he wanted to write a story about what happened, which in those days meant thinking up a nice long poem full of heroes, heroines, gods and monsters.

But Herodotus didn't want to do that . . . he'd read enough poems at school. No, he wanted to write about what really happened and why. So he travelled the world, talking to lots of people and asking questions like 'Why did the Persians invade Greece?', 'How come they lost?' and 'Why did they wear girly trousers instead of sensible skirts?'

Herodotus was the first 'historian'. After that everyone started asking questions about the past and they haven't stopped since. In fact we've got Herodotus to thank for this very book!

Our hero!

When he heard that they'd been betrayed, King Leonidas ordered most of Greek soldiers to retreat. But to give the others time to get away, he and a small group of Spartans stayed put in order to delay the enemy for as long as possible.

Persian soldiers poured through the little pass and soon the Spartans were surrounded on all sides. They fought to the last. When every spear was broken, they used their swords. When those had shattered, they used their bare hands, until after three days they were all dead.

But it had cost the Persians dearly – they had lost more than 20,000 men!

Now the Persian army swarmed into southern Greece and smashed Attica to bits. Even the mighty city of Athens was ransacked, though its inhabitants had been evacuated to the nearby island of Salamis.

It looked like the Greeks would be completely defeated and they'd have to suffer death and slavery and be forced to wear those daft trousers. But they had one final card to play – the Greek navy was itching for a fight.

And it was in the channel of water off Salamis that the navy made its last stand.

Battle of Salamis, 780 BC

Persians

Greeks

Xerxes, watching

SALAMIS

Persians

Did someone say salamis? I love salami!

SEA

GREEK SUPER-SHIPS

The Athenians had recently invested in 180 brand-new state-of-the-art battle ships. They were called 'triremes' or 'three-oarers' because there were three rows of oars on each side, powered by 170 oarsmen.

On the front of each ship was a massive wooden battering ram to punch holes in enemy boats, and a pair of big white eyes to make them look extra-scary!

The decks were full of rows of oarsmen; there wasn't any space on board for things like beds or kitchens or loos. So you can imagine the inside of a trireme got pretty disgusting!

Xerxes really wanted to finish the war and get home to Persia. So he sent his fleet of 1,200 Persian ships to wipe those cocky Greeks off the map. Unfortunately for him, there were too many Persian ships for the size of channel – they got all got jammed together!

The Greek triremes picked them off one by one – capturing or sinking over 200!

It was total victory!

Soon the Persians went home and never tried invading Greece again!

So what did the Greeks do next? They went back to fighting each other of course!

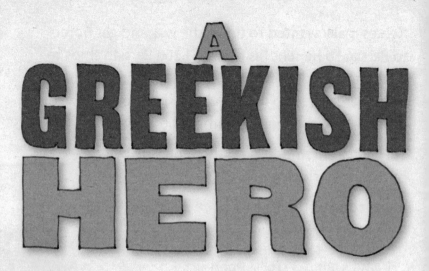

A GREEKISH HERO

OK – now we come to Alexander the Great. Alexander lived in the fourth century BC in Macedonia. Macedonia was the kingdom next door to ancient Greece. Now you might be thinking, If Alexander wasn't from Greece then what is he doing in a book about the Greeks . . . ?

If you are thinking that then well done, you're a very intelligent person who will go far and will probably end up being Prime Minister.

The answer is that even though they didn't live in a Greek city-state, the Macedonians still thought of themselves as Greek. They spoke Greek and believed in Greek gods. They even demanded to be allowed to join in the Olympic Games, which was a Greeks-only event. So they may not have been completely Greek, but they were certainly Greek-ish!!

I've got a whole chapter in this book, and I'm not even Greek!
That's because you're so great, Alexander.

Alexander's dad had been the King of Macedonia. He'd paid for young Alex to have the best Greek teachers who taught him all about Greece.

When Alexander took over from his dad as King, he wanted to carry on spreading 'Greek-ness' around the world. To do this, he started invading other countries and making them part of a single massive Greek-ish Empire.

THE ONE-EYED KING OF MACEDONIA

Alexander's dad was the famous and fierce King Philip II of Macedonia. He had led the Macedonian army to many victories – he had even lost an eye and had a massive scar across his cheek from being hit in the face with an arrow during a battle!

Philip had turned Macedonia from an insignificant little state on the edge of Greece into a powerful kingdom. The Greeks didn't like Philip much – they thought he was a barbarian in a bearskin who drank too much.

Still, that didn't stop him taking over Greece! One by one he took control of the Greek city-states and made himself 'Commander of the Greeks'.

A small ivory statue assumed to be Philip II.

STIG'S BRILLIANT GREEKS NO. 8: THE GREEK WHO WAS BRILLIANT AT BEING ANNOYING

Diogenes was very grumpy. One sunny day Alexander the Great, the most powerful man in the world, came to visit him. The conversation went something like this . . .

I have enormous respect for you, old man. Is there anything I can do for you?

Yes, I can't catch the rays with you standing in front of me. Move out the way!

OK, that was downright rude, but Diogenes' point was that you shouldn't be nice to someone just because they're rich and famous. He thought the worst thing anyone could be was two-faced. He was always shocking people, trying to teach them not to show off. He dressed like a beggar, weed on people he didn't like and even did a poo in the theatre. He was a bit scary and fairly disgusting, but he was very clever and was never frightened of powerful people. A lot of folk learned from him that they didn't need to be in awe of the rich Athenians. But however much he disliked showing off, wasn't he a bit of a show-off himself?

Alexander wasn't called 'Alexander the Great' because he had great hair or was great at doing 1,000-piece jigsaws.

He was called 'Great' because he was good at conquering places . . . in fact he was really, *really* great at it.

Why are there so many images of my lovely hair? Because I'm worth it!

Isn't he gorgeous?

What a hunk!

Huh!

What a show-off!

He made conquering countries look easy: first Persia, then Palestine, Syria, Afghanistan and Egypt were all defeated by Alexander's army. He never lost a single battle! He could conquer places with his eyes shut and one hand tied behind his back.

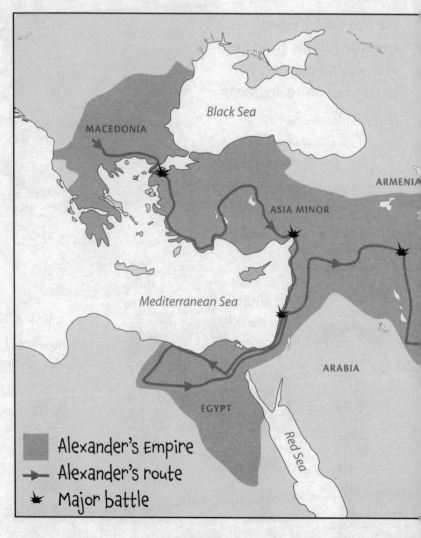

Black Sea

MACEDONIA

ARMENIA

ASIA MINOR

Mediterranean Sea

ARABIA

EGYPT

Red Sea

Alexander's Empire
Alexander's route
Major battle

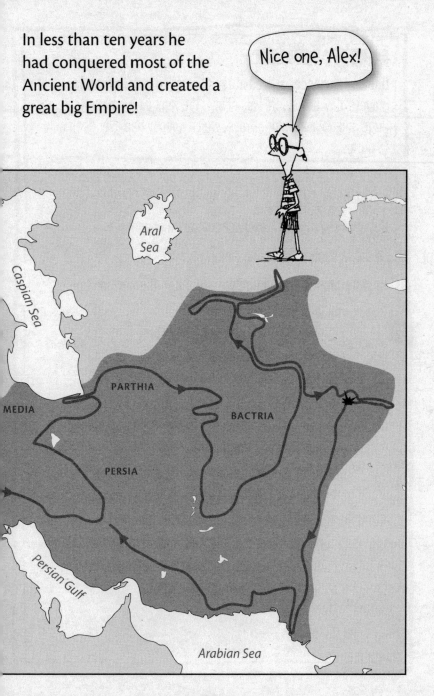

In less than ten years he had conquered most of the Ancient World and created a great big Empire!

Nice one, Alex!

A KNOTTY PROBLEM

One day Alexander arrived at the ancient city of Gordium in modern-day Turkey. He was shown the famous 'Gordian Knot', a large and ancient knot of rope, which nobody had ever been able to untie.

There was a legend that whoever could undo it would become the conqueror of Asia, so of course Alexander had to have a go.

But even the mighty Alexander couldn't manage it.

So did this mean he'd never conquer Asia?

No, he promptly drew his sword and sliced the knot in two.

Problem solved!

Which shows that Alexander was not only a clever chap but was also a pretty nifty swordsman!

ARE WE THERE YET?

Alexander's army loved him and would follow him anywhere – even when it meant trudging through a desert wasteland for weeks and weeks, dying of thirst and having to eat your horse.

In 325 BC Alexander began to cross the dreaded Gedrosian Desert. Nobody had ever brought an army through it successfully and he was determined to prove that he could!

To avoid the heat the troops marched at night, but supplies were short and both men and animals started collapsing from thirst and exhaustion. Anybody too sick or tired was left behind – the army had to keep moving to get to the other side of the desert as fast as possible. Some soldiers ended up butchering their own horses and eating them just to stay alive!

Don't even think about it!

Alexander's army finally made it across, but hundreds had died, their bodies left behind to be swallowed up by the desert sands.

OX-HEAD

Alexander's horse was almost as famous as him.

When Alexander was thirteen, his dad bought a massive black horse with a white star on his forehead. But the horse turned out to be so wild that nobody could ride him. The King told Alexander that if he could tame the horse, he could keep him. To everybody's surprise, Alexander managed it!

But he didn't give his new pet a romantic name like 'Black Beauty' – no, he named him 'Bucephalus' or 'Ox-head' because he had a huge head. He may have been an odd-looking horse, but Alexander loved him very much and rode him everywhere.

Eventually 'Ox–head' was killed in a battle. Alexander was gutted, so he founded a new city on the spot and named it Bucephala. The first (and only) city to be named after a horse!

THE END OF THE WORLD

Eventually Alexander's army refused to go any further east – they'd reached India and they thought if they went any further they'd fall off the end of the world. (They didn't know there was all of China further east!)

GOING BANANAS

In India Alexander and his army discovered strange bendy yellow fruit growing on tall trees and they tasted delicious. In fact they were so yummy that the Greeks brought a load of them back home. So it's Alexander the Great that we have to thank for the banana!

Alexander agreed to start heading home.

Unfortunately, he never made it back – he died mysteriously of a fever in 323 BC. We don't really know what killed him – some people say he was poisoned, others think he died of malaria or typhoid fever . . . (or perhaps he just ate a dodgy banana?).

He was only 32 but he had conquered more places than any other person before or since!

In northern India Alexander won a battle against war elephants.
After that his men didn't want to carry on any further.

On his deathbed, his officers came to Alexander and asked him who should take over the Empire he'd created? To which he responded, '*The strongest.*'

So all his generals were left to fight it out among themselves!

In the end they chose to split it up because it was so large – each general took a separate bit of the empire: one took Egypt, one took the lands of East Asia, one took the area of modern Turkey and one took Macedonia. As for the Greek cities – well, most of them went back to fighting among themselves! (What did you expect?)

Aristotle was just about the cleverest Greek of all. Some people said he knew everything it was possible to know. That's probably a bit of an exaggeration, but he was certainly in demand. The King of Macedonia even employed him as teacher to his son Alexander.

Aristotle was interested in everything – the stars, foreign countries, books, poetry, but particularly in animals and nature. People like Socrates and Pythagoras got pretty hung up about what was real; in fact whether anything was real at all.

I'm the best thinker there is . . . I think.

But Aristotle said he saw real things every day – the rain falling, chickens laying eggs, people sneezing, that kind of thing.

He was good at writing too. People called his words 'a river of gold'.

He wasn't always right. He thought the Earth was the centre of the universe, that heavy objects fall faster than light ones, and that women have more teeth than men.

Blimey!

But he had the courage to tell Alexander the Great that kings and queens were pointless unless they were better behaved than all their subjects put together – and I reckon that makes him not only very smart, but also very brave!

WE'RE ALL GREEKS NOW

Alexander's massive Empire may not have lasted very long but he brought 'Greek-ness' to the whole world.

During his travels, he had founded more than 70 cities all across his Empire. The generals who took over from him built even more!

Greetings from Egypt

These cities were run by Greeks and had all the things – like gymnasiums, theatres and temples – that Greek cities had.

Pretty soon, lots of Greeks were moving out of Greece and into these new cities – why stick around in boring

Greetings from Sicily

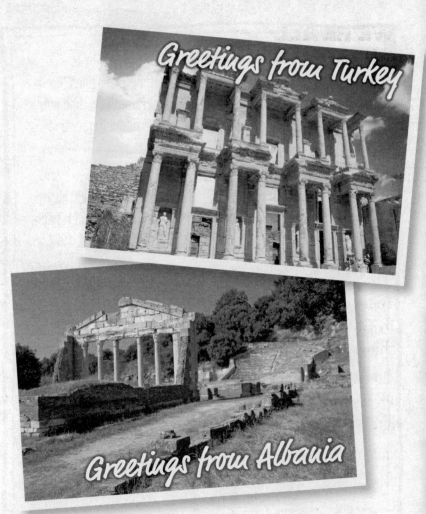

Greetings from Turkey

Greetings from Albania

old Greece when you could live it up in exotic places like . . . Alexandria (named after who? You guessed it) in Egypt?

The Greeks brought with them their language, their fashions, their money and their ideas. Famous scientists, philosophers and artists came from all over the world to study Greek documents in its world-famous library.

THE LIBRARY OF ALEXANDRIA

In the Ancient World there was no internet, no magazines, no newspapers and no printed books. So if you wanted to find out anything you either had to ask somebody or find a library and look it up in a scroll.

The library at Alexandria was built by one of Alexander's Generals, Ptolemy (pronounced 'Tol-em-ee') in about 300 BC. It was the largest library in the Ancient World. People said it had a copy of every book (or 'scroll') ever written!

The rulers of Alexandria were so proud of their library that they'd do anything to get hold of books for it. Sometimes they stole them off ships visiting the city. Once they asked to 'borrow' a load of rare books from the city of Athens and never returned them!

Great, we've finally got the full set of Tony Robinsons!

It would take rather a long time to read every book ever written. Unfortunately, even if you wanted to try it, you couldn't. The library at Alexandria was burned down when the city was attacked and many of its books were lost forever.

It was an accident, I promise!

Which is a real shame – just think of all the stuff that might have been in those books . . . an invention for a time machine perhaps? Or the recipe for the elixir of life? Or maybe just an ancient Greek version of this book?

One of the people blamed for burning down the library was Julius Caesar – the famous Roman general. He attacked Alexandria in 48 BC as part of his campaign to take over Egypt.

GRACE'S BRILLIANT GREEKS NO. 1: THE GREEK WHO WAS BRILLIANT AT TELLING STORIES

Homer was a blind poet who told really exciting tales . . .

> Hang on! Isn't this the bloke who was *my* Brilliant Greek No. 1?

Well yes, but some people think Homer was a woman. So I'm putting him/her in twice.

> But weren't Greek women supposed to stay at home and not do anything except have babies?

That's certainly what a lot of ancient writers tell us. But it can't have been completely true. There's a woman poet called Sappho whose poems are just as good as any written by the male Greek poets.

There are a lot of smart goddesses in the ancient tales too, like Athena and Artemis, who do all sorts of clever stuff, and you get the feeling their characters were based on the swanky celebs of the time.

We can't prove whether Homer was a Home-him or a Home-her, but there must have been loads of Greek women around who were just as brilliant as the brilliant blokes – we just don't know their names!

ROME RULES

The Romans had read about what Alexander the Great had achieved and thought that creating a global Empire sounded like a great idea! So they copied him.

Slowly they started taking over the world – first they conquered Greece and Macedonia, then they moved into Asia and Egypt. All these places became Roman provinces.

Countries that for centuries had been ruled by the Greeks, started to be ruled by the Romans.

But it wasn't the end of Greek-ness . . .

The Romans were big fans of Greek stuff. They took home with them Greek works of art and Greek books; they adopted Greek gods and employed Greek teachers. Some Romans even toured Greece and studied in Athens.

And the Romans passed Greek ideas on to us!

Next time you walk down a street and see a building with lots of fancy columns on the front, next time you go to a **theatre** or **write a story**, next time you use a **calculator**, look at the **stars** or eat a **banana**, next time you **pick up a book** because you're really interested in finding out what's inside it – remember that you're following in the footsteps of the ancient Greeks!

TIMELINE

6500 BC	The first farmers start to settle down in Greece
3300 BC	The Sumerians, who lived in modern Iraq, develop writing
3000 BC	The ancient Egyptian civilization gets going
1500 BC	A great palace stands at Knossos – could this be the home of King Minos and the Minotaur?
1180 BC	The Trojan Wars happen (according to some people!)
776 BC	The Olympic Games begin
740 BC (ish)	The Greeks develop their own alphabet
700 BC (ish)	Some Greeks settle in Sicily and southern Italy, while the Etruscans start a little civilization further north in Italy.
621 BC	Draco the Athenian writes down his very strict laws
610–575 BC	Sappho knocks out some fantastic poetry, despite being a woman (shock!)
548 BC	The Temple of Apollo at Delphi is destroyed
534/3 BC	Thespis becomes the world's first actor, and wins a talent contest in Athens
525 BC	The Persians take over Egypt
525–500 BC	Pythagoras gets excited about numbers
520 BC (ish)	Athenians start making their own coins with owls on
509 BC (ish)	The Romans kick out the Etruscans and start a new republic
507 BC	Cleisthenes comes up with a great new idea – democracy!

490 BC	The Emperor Darius of Persia sends an army to invade Attica: for 20 years, Darius and his son Xerxes keep trying to bash the Greeks, but eventually have to give up
484 BC (ish)	Herodotus the historian is born. A few years later, he starts asking some pretty good questions . . .
480 BC	At the Battle of Thermopylae the Spartans prove how hard they are
460–377 BC	Dr Hippocrates works on his bedside manner
450 BC	The Athenians build the Parthenon, a massive marble temple to the gods with a 40-foot-high golden statue of Athena inside
445–429 BC	Pericles rules Athens, which he turns into a great city (he also sends the Spartans packing, twice)
431 BC	A major bust-up between Athens and Sparta begins, called the Peloponnesian War
399 BC	Socrates is ordered to drink poison, and for once he does as he's told
384–322 BC	Aristotle thinks great thoughts (and also teaches Alexander the Great)
323 BC	Alexander the Great dies at the age of 32; he's been busy!
300 BC	Ptolemy builds the Library at Alexandria, which holds over half a million books
200 BC	By this time, the Romans have conquered the Greeks
1800s	Lord Elgin swipes some lovely souvenirs from the Parthenon

QUIZ

1 Who thought they were the 'best people' in Athens?

2 Where did Elgin put his marbles?

3 What did Hippocrates suggest you do with your earwax?

4 What drew the crowds to the hill called the Pnyx?

5 What clever gadget could the Greeks make with just a pot of water?

6 What did Draco think should happen to lazy people?

7 What was the last thing left in Pandora's box?

8 How do you break into a Greek house?

9 What sort of fishy Valentine might impress an ancient Greek?

10 How did the Athenians kill Socrates?

11 What should you wear for your ancient Greek PE lesson?

12 What did the Athenians put on their coins?

13 What came out of Greek vending machines?

14 What did the Helots do for the Spartans?

15 What colour was a Spartan school uniform?

16 Which god avoided being eaten by his dad?

17 What was the Olympic sport of 'total combat' called?

18 What did the Olympic hero Milo of Croton carry around with him?

19 What did Archimedes use to make his death ray?

20 What strange new garment did the trendy Persians wear?

21 What does the word 'hoplite' mean?

22 Who was killed by a flying tortoise?

23 What did Diogenes ask Alexander the Great to do for him?

ANSWERS 1) The 'aristoi', or aristocrats. 2) In London. 3) Eat it. 4) Not the view – elections! 5) A clock. 6) Death! 7) Hope. 8) Dig through the wall. 9) An octopus. 10) With poison. 11) Nothing at all! 12) An owl with olive leaves. 13) Holy water. 14) Everything – they were their slaves! 15) Red – to hide the bloodstains! 16) Zeus. 17) Pankration. 18) A bull. 19) Mirrors. 20) Trousers. 21) Armoured. 22) Aeschylus the playwright. 23) Move out of the way of the sun.

For Holly . . .
This book is for **Holly Shepherd-Robinson**. She's only two years old,
so she can't read it yet. But she can nibble at it, wear it as a hat,
or drop it from a great height so it goes *bang!* on the floor.

Hopefully in about five years' time she'll try to read it. But by then
it'll be so dog-eared and manky and stained with tomato ketchup
that she'll have to buy her own copy, and I'll make about 17p!

. . . and Jess
It's also for **Jessica Cobb**, whose brains are bigger than a
double-decker bus. In fact, if she didn't stick her head out of the
window when she's on the way home, she'd squash all the other
passengers. I couldn't have written the book without her.

Picture
Credits

left to right
t = top; b = bottom; r = right; l = left; c = centre

Shutterstock images: 161 A_Belov; 164 Andrei Nekrassov;
170 marcello mura; 180 Croato; 185t katad; 185b Jiri Pavlik;
187 edo; 191 Anibal Trejo; 193t Matthew Collingwood;
193b Justin Black; 195 Bill Perry; 197 meunierd; 200 HENX;
201 Kevin H. Knuth; 213 Elnur; 217 Kate Connes; 218 Pete Kilmek; 223 Offscreen;
226 F.C.G.; 238 Vladimir Korostyshevskiy; 244 Ian MacDonald; 245 Jaime Pharr;
248 Kamira; 248 Aquila; 249 Andrei Nekrassov; 254 javarman; 255 Vladimir
Korostyshevskiy; 261 Ross Ellet; 263 riekephotos; 266t Kenneth V. Pilon;
271 alessandro0770; 272 PLRANG; 273 Lagui; 277 Gelia; 279 Faraways; 280 majeczka;
281 Olga Matseyko; 282 Clara; 283 nito; 287 Teerapun; 288 pseudolongino;
294 Brian Maudsley; 295 imagestalk; 302 WitR; 304 imagestalk; 305t Simon Smith;
305b Kenneth V. Pilon; 306 Vitaly Titov & Maria Sidelnikova and Eon Images:
250, 265, 269 and 291; KF Archive 186, 269 and 274r; Loicwood 173; Marie-Lan
Nguyen/Wikimedia Commons 274l.

Hi! We're the Curiosity Crew. You may spot us hanging about in this book, checking stuff out.

It's about the Roman Empire, which in ancient times ruled pretty much all the known world for hundreds of years. That's impressive, particularly when you think that Rome started off in about 750 BC as an ordinary little farming village.

Although, actually, there's a much better story about how the whole Roman thing began, and it's pretty wild . . . that's if you believe it!

Read on to find out . . .

Stig   Nits   Grace   Peewee   Jojo

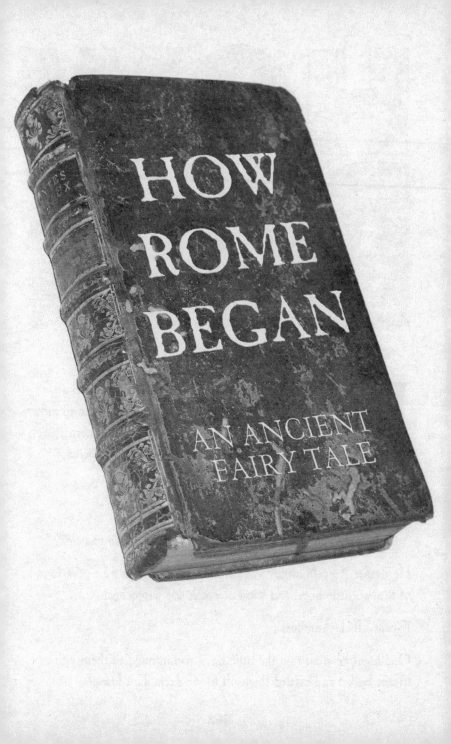

HOW ROME BEGAN

AN ANCIENT FAIRY TALE

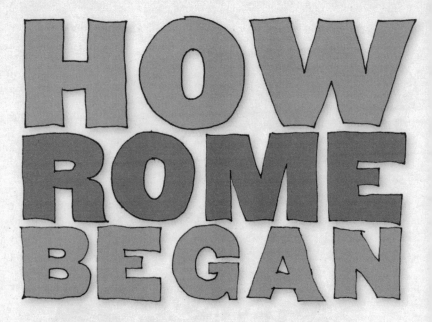

HOW ROME BEGAN

L ong, long ago in the faraway country of Italy there lived a
beautiful young priestess called Rhea Silvia who began to grow
fat. After six months she had a belly the size of a watermelon,
and her uncle Amulius grabbed her by the sleeve and whispered,
'You're going to have a baby!'

'No,' said Rhea Silvia. 'I'm going to have two babies.'

And she did. Three months later Rhea Silvia gave birth to twins.

Her father King Numitor was naturally very upset, but he grew fond
of the two little boys, and soon everyone was happy again . . .

Except Uncle Amulius.

One night he crept into the little boys' room, bundled them into a
wicker basket and carried them off to the deep, dark forest.

'You have brought shame on our family,' he hissed. 'So now you must die.' And he tipped them out on to the musty, dusty leaves, leaving them to their fate.

All night they lay there. They didn't cry — they were brave little boys. But they were very hungry.

Then towards morning there was a snuffling sound, and the pad of soft paws, and a great grey wolf loped out of the surrounding trees.

Mummy?

The wolf picked up one twin in her sharp, white teeth and carried him back to her den. Then she returned, picked up the other one, and brought him back to her den too.

But she didn't harm them. Her cubs had recently died in a tragic chariot accident, and she was full of milk and without any babies to love.

So she looked after the little boys and raised them as her own. She chased away the hungry badgers when they came too close to the den, and she covered them with the musty, dusty leaves when they were cold in winter. And they became strong and clever, and as wily as . . . err . . . wolves.

Stop! Stop this story right now!

Until one day, when they were eight years old, and their Wolf Mother had died and gone to Wolf Heaven, they were discovered by shepherds and taken back to the shepherds' village. There they were given a hut to live in, clothes to wear and names too. One was named Romulus and the other Remus.

This isn't true, you know.

By the time the boys had grown to manhood, Rhea Silvia's father was no longer king. Wicked Uncle Amulius had seized the crown, and had thrown Numitor into a damp and unhygienic dungeon. In fact Amulius threw almost anyone he could into that deep and unhygienic dungeon, and one day when Remus had strayed too near the palace while looking for a lost lamb, Amulius grabbed him and threw him in for trespassing.

The young man soon befriended Numitor, who told him his two grandsons had once been stolen from him. Fortunately Remus had an unusual birthmark behind his knee, and one afternoon Numitor saw it. He suddenly realised who Remus was — his long-lost grandson!

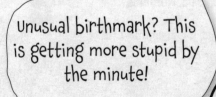

Unusual birthmark? This is getting more stupid by the minute!

Meanwhile Romulus had raised an army of brave shepherds who marched to the palace, broke down the door, seized Amulius, chopped him into bite-sized nuggets and threw him in the moat.

When the shepherds released Remus, he told them that he and his brother were heirs to the throne. The whole city cheered, held a three-day party and offered Romulus and Remus the crown. But they refused.

'Our grandfather Numitor is the rightful king,' they said. 'He shall rule here. We will set off and found a new city.'

So their mother Rhea Silvia brushed a tear from her eye, packed their lunch boxes and kissed them goodbye, and off they went, accompanied by the shepherds and a few scruffy, runaway slaves.

Ignore this, young reader! It's a pack of lies.

The Romans like to believe it, though!

After several days they came to two hills. One was called the Palatine Hill. 'We'll build our city here!' said Romulus.

The other was called the Aventine Hill. 'No, we'll build our city here,' said Remus.

And they began to argue. Romulus dug a trench and Remus filled it in again.

Remus lay some foundations, and Romulus walked all over the wet concrete in his big boots.

Romulus built a brick wall, and Remus kicked it over.

This was too much for Romulus. He picked up a rusty shovel, hit Remus on the head, and Remus fell down dead.

'We shall build my city here on the Palatine Hill,' announced Romulus. 'And what is more we will name it after me.

'It will be called Rome, and we shall be known as the Romans!'

Romans! Romans! Yeah, yeah, we're the Romans!

But there was a small problem . . .

'We're all men,' said the shepherds and the scruffy, runaway slaves. 'You can't start a city with ALL men.'

'Then I'll fetch some women,' Romulus replied, and straight away, he marched down into the valley and captured all the women who lived there. He brought them back to Rome and made them become Roman wives, even though some of them were extremely annoyed.

From above, Mars looked down on his son's city and he loved it. He would make it the most powerful place in the land . . . and that's how Rome began.

No, it's not! Rome was NOT founded by a badly behaved boy who'd been brought up by a wolf, but by a sophisticated people called the Etruscans. They taught the Romans mathematics, architecture and loads of other stuff. Even the word 'Roman' is an Etruscan word.

169

THE SONS OF MARS
PART ONE

By 300 BC, the city of Rome had built up a powerful army. Roman men reckoned they were as good at fighting as Romulus's dad, Mars the god of war, so they called themselves 'The Sons of Mars'.

They were **incredibly** proud of their army – and you can't blame them. It was a lean, mean fighting machine.

If it had been a football team, it would have been Chelsea, Man U and Barcelona combined. It would have won the League, the Cup and Champions League not just once, but for **centuries**.

Roman centurions, who were top army officers, wore these fancy helmets.

INSULTS ACROSS THE SEA

So Rome went to war and once it had taken over all the little kingdoms around it . . .

Including the land of the Etruscans!

. . . it started eyeing up massive places further afield.

One of the most powerful was **Carthage** – a city on the North African coast, just across the other side of the Mediterranean Sea. Rome hated Carthage and Carthage hated Rome, but for a long time neither was strong enough to crush the other. So they just sort of glared at one another and shouted insults.

You're a wimp!

Kiss that!

CRAZY HANNIBAL

Then a new young general took command of Carthage's army. His name was Hannibal and he wasn't going to take any more Roman aggravation. He decided not just to attack Rome, but to **invade** it.

But rather than popping across to Italy in a few boats, he sailed to Spain. Then he marched his army through Spain, across France and over the Alps, the big mountains that divide France and Italy!

This came as a bit of a shock to the Romans – who didn't expect anyone to be **crazy** enough to climb over a massive range of snow-covered mountains to get at them.

But that's exactly why Hannibal did it . . . not because he was crazy (OK, well maybe a bit) but because he knew the Romans wouldn't be expecting it!

Here Hannibal is holding the Roman standard (a stick with a big symbol at the end). He's turned it upside down, to show he beat the Romans.

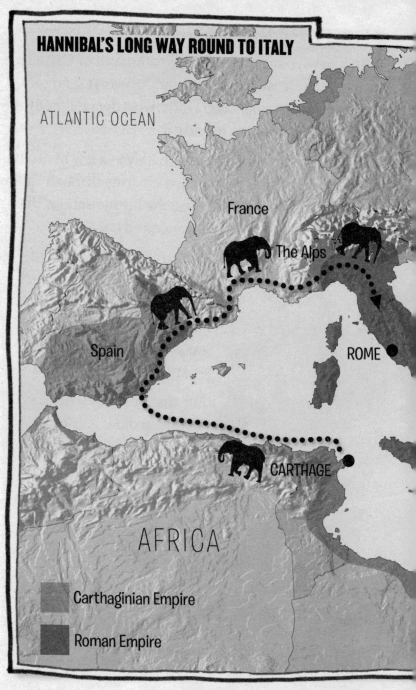

HANNIBAL'S LONG WAY ROUND TO ITALY

ATLANTIC OCEAN

France

The Alps

Spain

ROME

CARTHAGE

AFRICA

Carthaginian Empire

Roman Empire

WAR ELEPHANTS

The army Hannibal took with him over the Alps included more than 30 **elephants**.

This may seem a bit weird, but ancient armies were quite keen on using elephants in battle. There's nothing like hundreds of angry jumbos charging at the enemy to make them think twice!

But however impressive they were, Hannibal's elephants weren't much use to him. Most of them died on their way through the mountains and the ones which didn't were pretty knackered . . . but then so would you be if you'd just walked all the way from Africa.

The Romans decided to send a vast army of 80,000 soldiers to face Hannibal at Cannae in south-east Italy.

Unfortunately for Rome, Hannibal was very good at coming up with sneaky and surprising ways to win. He'd already won a battle at sea by throwing barrels of poisonous snakes into the enemy boats. That's the kind of commander he was – you had to watch him because you never knew what he was going to do next!

Realizing he was outnumbered, Hannibal made sure that when the Romans advanced, his army deliberately gave way. The Romans charged forward and the edges of Hannibal's army closed around them in a big circle.

The Roman army was trapped and Hannibal's troops attacked them from all sides. More than 50,000 Roman soldiers are said to have been slaughtered – one writer said that the Carthaginians killed them at the rate of 600 men a minute until night fell.

BATTLE OF CANNAE

Date: 216 BC

Roman Army: 80,000

Carthaginians: 50,000 (including a handful of very tired elephants)

Score: 10-nil to Carthage (or 'a draw' if you're a Roman)

Man of the match: Super-striker Hannibal

Cannae was a big defeat for the Romans, like being relegated from the Premier League or losing in the first round of the cup.

Anyone else would have blamed the ref, or gone home to have a bit of a cry . . . but not the Romans.

No – they absolutely refused to accept that they were beaten. The way they saw it – if the city of Rome was still standing, then they **hadn't** been defeated!

On the one hand this is a bit mental, but on the other hand it explains why it was so difficult to defeat the Romans. Unless you marched into the city of Rome itself, set fire to it, crushed all the buildings into little bits and stomped up and down on the blackened

Let's go home, Jumbo.

Sure thing, Dumbo.

remains, there were always going to be Romans shouting *'Come on, chaps! We're not beaten yet!'*

And sure enough, within a year the Romans had got a new army together, and headed for Carthage. Hannibal was forced to leave Italy to defend his homeland.

Once again he decided to rely on war elephants. But this time, the Romans were ready for him – when the elephants charged, the Roman soldiers blew loud horns, causing them to panic and trample on their own troops. The Roman army encircled Hannibal's army and **destroyed** it. Rome may have lost the Battle of Cannae, but it won the war!

Losers! Losers!

So am I!

A model of Ancient Rome as it looked two thousand years ago, in the first century AD. Pretty impressive, huh?

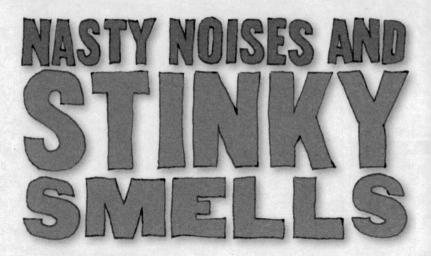

NASTY NOISES AND STINKY SMELLS

Most people in ancient times lived in little villages. The biggest excitement they got in a day was if someone fell over in the mud, or if a pig got the hiccups! But not in Rome . . .

Thanks to the success of its army, Rome was soon the largest city in the world and home to over one million people – a sprawling mass of houses, temples, theatres, baths and shops.

If you were a visitor from one of those tiny villages, your jaw would have practically hit the pavement at the sheer size and magnificence of the place!

HANDS OVER YOUR EARS

It was jam-packed. Most Romans lived crowded together in apartment blocks divided by narrow streets full of traffic and people.

And it was incredibly noisy. There were the piercing shouts of street sellers, the racket of wooden carts, the plink and plonk of musicians, knife grinders setting your teeth on edge, and the bashing and crashing of carpenters and metalsmiths.

SHAPES IN THE ASH

The ancient city of Pompeii in southern Italy tells us loads about what Roman houses looked like, what type of work Romans did and what they ate.

On 24 August 79 AD, a volcano called Mount Vesuvius erupted and buried Pompeii in hot ash and lava. Houses, people and animals were covered in the ash, which cooled and hardened like rock.

1,700 years later, the city was rediscovered and dug out. Everything looked like it did the day the volcano erupted. Bread was still in the ovens, food in the restaurants, tools in the workshops and furniture in the houses.

There was even ancient graffiti written on some of the walls, and it was the same type of stuff people write today like:

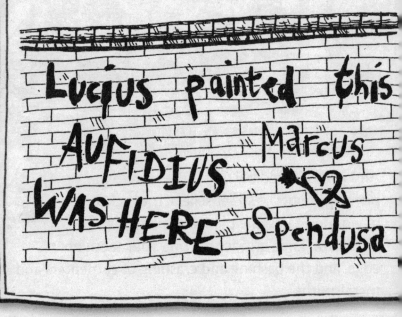

Lucius painted this

AUFIDIUS WAS HERE

Marcus ♥ Spendusa

People caught fleeing from the eruption, frozen in time.

Bodies had decomposed but left shapes in the hardened ash. Experts filled these holes with plaster to create statues of the people and animals killed in the disaster.

There are still lots more things to find in Pompeii. The only problem is that digging it up might destroy it. Some people are worried that the buildings are starting to crumble and break. Plus, lots of tourists visit Pompeii and walk all over it chipping off bits to take home as souvenirs!

A plaster cast of a man trying to protect his eyes from the ash.

HANDS OVER YOUR MOUTHS

Apart from the noise, another massive problem was the smell. With so many people living and working close together, the streets quickly filled with rubbish, rotting food and lots of poo.

Luckily, the Romans had a system to wash it away!

Phew!

Ack

Think of all the reasons you need water – drinking, cooking, cleaning, washing... that's a lot of wet stuff, isn't it? But times it by a million and that's how much water Rome needed every day. Unfortunately, people couldn't use the water from the local

How to build an aqueduct.

river because it got really dirty and they'd have found themselves guzzling dishwater and other people's wee.

So the Romans built 'aqueducts' – long channels for bringing in fresh water from springs outside the city. Being Romans, they didn't mess around if there was a problem. When there was a valley in the way, they just built a bridge with a channel inside it to carry the water.

At one time Rome had nine aqueducts delivering 46 million gallons of water to the city every day. It collected in big reservoirs, then flowed through pipes into fountains, baths and private villas all round the city. Once it had been used, the dirty water from the streets, houses and toilets flowed back out of the city in sewer pipes.

MAKING THE RULES – PART ONE

Building things like sewers and public toilets was very complicated, and the Romans needed a strong government to persuade people to cough up the money for all that digging and plumbing. But they were fed up with having kings like Romulus telling them what to do; it was their money, and they wanted to be able to decide how to spend it. So they turned their city into a 'Republic', which basically means they ran it themselves.

In charge was the Senate, 300 posh people who claimed they were related to the very earliest Roman shepherds . . .

HANDS OVER YOUR NOSES

Many Romans didn't have their own loo, but you could pay a small fee to use a public toilet, where you sat on a bench and did your business through a hole into a channel below. It wasn't very private – you just sat between lots of other people doing the same thing, and when you wanted to wipe your bum someone passed you a sponge on a stick!

Roman toilets could sit up to 60 people – yikes!

MAKING THE RULES – PART TWO

The Roman Republic was really successful – all Roman citizens felt they had a say in how Rome was run and were really proud of it. And to remind everyone of that fact, the letters **SPQR** (which stood for **'Senatus Populus Que Romanus'** or **'The Senate and People of Rome'**) were stamped not only on Roman coins, but on Roman buildings, Roman paving stones and even Roman drainpipes!

A Roman mosaic – it's that wolf and the twins again.

I'm certainly proud to be a Roman.

So am I. I've even had a reminder stamped on my head!

SPQR

The poor didn't have enough money to go to public toilets, so they used a pot instead. When it was full, they were supposed to take it out and empty it into a sewer, but lots of people couldn't be bothered . . . and chucked the contents out of the window on to the streets below!

Run for it!

GET YOUR WHITES WHITE . . .

Not all Rome's wee went down a sewer or over people's heads. Ever wondered how the Romans kept their togas so white?

They sent them off to the fuller's shop to be washed, dyed, rinsed and dried. The chemicals in human urine are very good for cleaning cloth, so the fullers soaked people's clothes in vats of pee, which they bought from the city's public toilets!

A NICE LONG SOAK

Romans were big fans of baths and bathing. There was nothing they liked more than taking a long soak in a hot bath and having a good scrub. But not many people could afford their own bath.

So big public baths were built for everyone to use. These were a bit like a health club – they had pools, hot tubs, saunas, steam rooms and gyms. There were places to get a massage or a haircut, quiet corners where you could read, and there were even people selling fast food if you felt a bit peckish.

Inside, you could have a cold bath (a '*frigidarium*'), a warm bath (a '*tepidarium*') and a hot bath (a '*caldarium*') with water heated by a furnace. Often you would use all of them, one after the other!

You didn't use soap – instead you rubbed your skin with oil and cleaned it off with a metal scraper. This took off all the dirt, dead skin and sweat. If you were rich, your slaves would do it for you. And no one wanted to be hairy. So you hired someone to pluck out your body hair with a pair of tweezers!

There were hundreds of baths in Rome, and they were usually packed. People went there to hang out with their friends, have business meetings or just chill out.

Sounds great! Let's whizz back to Ancient Rome for a quick splash and a soak.

Err . . . no, best not! The water got pretty disgusting – full of hair, fast food and dead skin. Blurrgghh!

ICK

THE SONS OF MARS

PART TWO

When Rome was just a medium-sized city, its army was made up of ordinary farmers who bought a shield and helmet, then took time off work to march around being soldiers for a bit. But once Rome got really big this became a serious problem. It was all very well asking farmers to leave their work to fight the odd battle, but war was becoming a full-time occupation.

The farmers needed to be doing other things like mucking out their cows, sowing their seeds and pulling up their turnips. They couldn't just go off gallivanting around the world all the time, bashing foreigners.

So Rome started to pay people to fight. Then, once they had a decent wage, a shiny new kit and three hot meals a day, Roman soldiers happily spent years travelling the world beating people up to their hearts' content!

Some bloke dressed as a Roman soldier. If he was the real thing, he'd be carrying a lot more stuff!

DO THE MATHS

The Roman army was divided into **legions** of about 5,000 men.
Start counting!

Each legion was divided into ten **cohorts** (480 men).

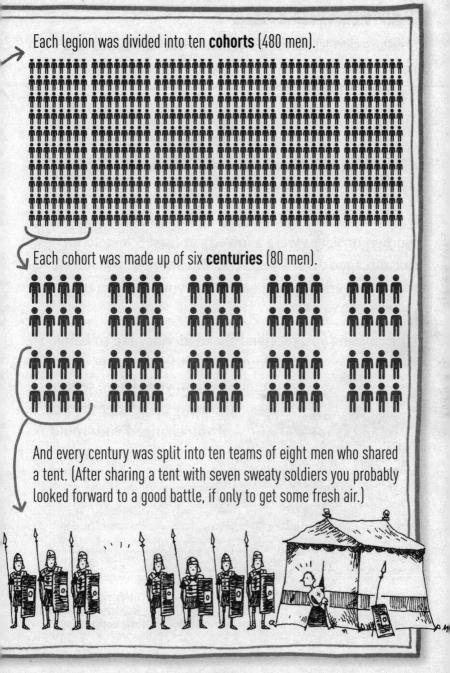

Each cohort was made up of six **centuries** (80 men).

And every century was split into ten teams of eight men who shared a tent. (After sharing a tent with seven sweaty soldiers you probably looked forward to a good battle, if only to get some fresh air.)

TATTS AND TAGS

Soldiers signed up for 25 years. In ancient times you were lucky to live past 40, so this was pretty much signing up for life!

You didn't have to be from Rome to be a soldier – they came from all the places the Romans had invaded. Lots of the soldiers who served in Britain were from North Africa.

If you wanted to join up, you had to be a free man (no women or slaves were allowed), at least 5 feet 10 inches tall and aged 20–25 years old. But some units weren't that picky, and if you were big for your age you might get in at 14 or 15.

After joining you received a lead identity tag to hang round your neck, and sometimes you also got a tattoo on your hand, so that the army could identify you if you changed your mind and tried to run away.

Soldiers still wear identity tags around their necks today.

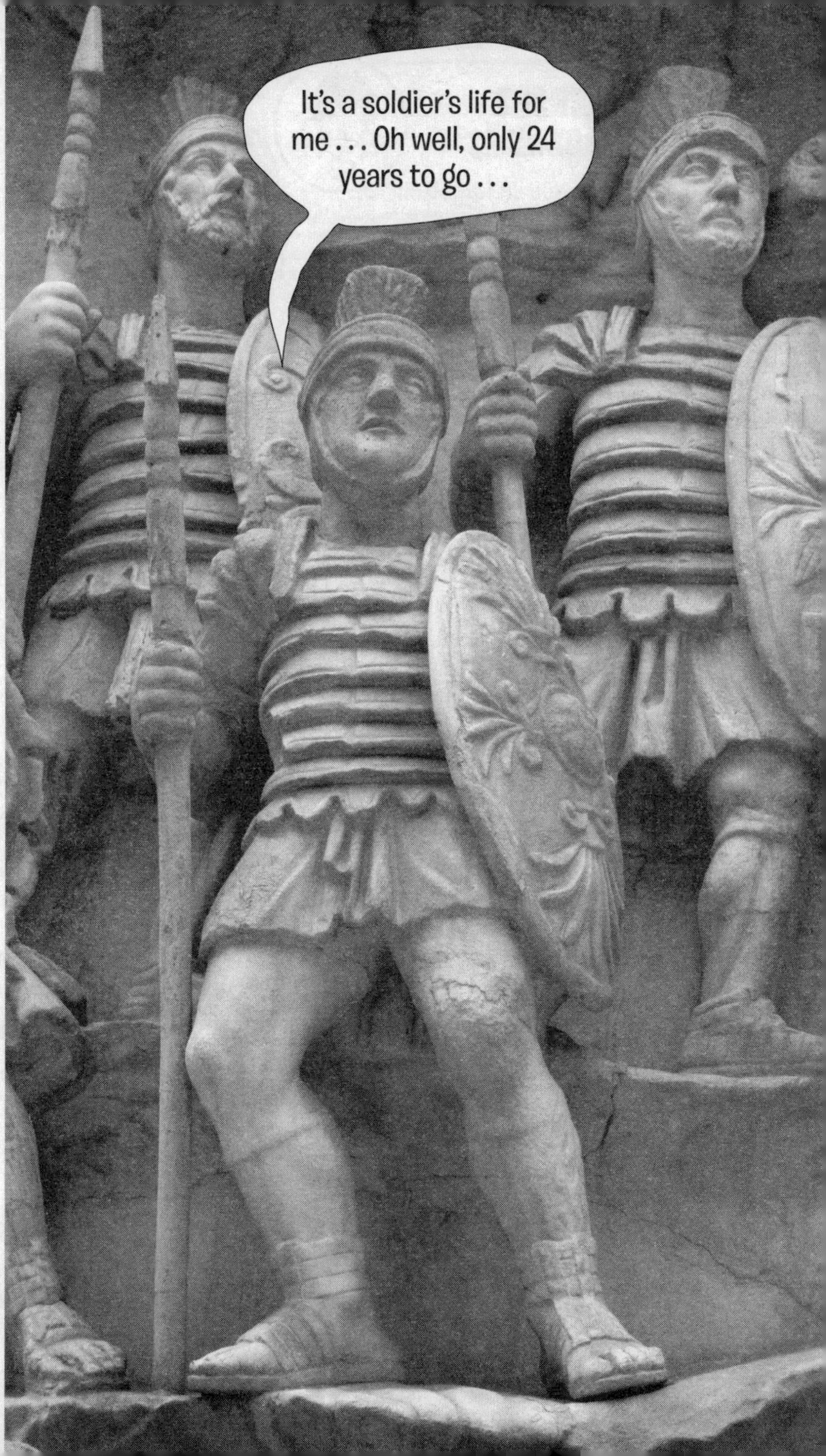
It's a soldier's life for me . . . Oh well, only 24 years to go . . .

STIG'S PICTURE OF A TYPICAL SON OF MARS

That's a soldier, if you've forgotten!

Helmet – called 'galea'. Made from metal with flaps to protect your cheeks and the back of your neck. You could clip a horsehair crest to the top to look extra impressive, but that was definitely not to be worn in battle because it was too easy for the enemy to grab it and get you in a headlock!

Dagger – called a 'pugio'. Handy for when you saw a large angry barbarian storming towards you.

Shield – called a 'scutum'. Made from wood, covered in animal skin and with a large iron knob on the front (a 'boss') for stopping blows.

Big stick – called a 'pilum', with a metal point on the end. Could be thrown up to 100 feet. If it didn't kill the enemy, he'd spend the rest of the battle trying to get this lethal weapon out of his shield.

Mail armour – made of lots of metal links joined together to make a sort of heavy metal jumper.

Another sort of armour – called 'lorica segmentata'. Made of overlapping strips of metal attached to leather straps.

Padding – under the armour. Because metal armour might save your life but it was really uncomfortable!

Sword – called a 'gladius'. It was double-edged, which meant you could just wave it about and be sure to do a bit of damage somewhere.

Boots – called 'caligas'. These were sandals with metal studs in the bottom for added grip (also good for stomping on the enemy, but not for chasing him across a marble floor, as you would probably skid, fall over and stab yourself).

COWS FOR TARGET PRACTICE

If you were a new recruit in the army, you had to train every day.

You're probably thinking – hey, being trained to fight doesn't sound so bad; learning how to kick ass . . . I could do that.

Well, it's true that Roman soldiers learned to fight; they practised with heavy wooden swords and shields, fought mock battles and even used the heads of dead cows as target practice. Yes, really.

But this was only part of their training. They were also taught another important skill . . . the art of walking a long way while carrying lots of heavy things.

The Roman army was on the go from dawn to dusk, marching from place to place and pitching their tents at the end of each day. And when they weren't marching or fighting, the soldiers were building things like roads and forts.

So they were specially trained to march 18 miles in five hours in full armour while carrying all their kit – including their weapons, shield, food, spare clothes, a short spade, a tool kit, a cooking pot, a big stone for grinding corn and two wooden stakes (in case they needed to put up a protective fence round their camp).

The whole lot weighed about 30 kilograms – that's the same weight as an average eight-year-old. So if you're eight, you could tell your friends that you're as heavy as a Roman soldier's backpack. Then you could get them to see if they're tough enough to carry you 18 miles. My bet is most of them would collapse after 18 metres!

To make sure the recruits were good at walking and carrying, they were made to practise **a lot**. And a burly bloke with a big stick marched behind them to whack anyone who wanted to go home early.

In fact you got whacked for virtually everything you did wrong, except for really serious crimes which were punished by death. Soldiers who ran away in battle were crucified (nailed to a wooden cross and left to die) or were thrown to wild animals, while soldiers who went to sleep while on

Soldiers, from the left – number . . .

One!

Two!

Three!

Four!

Five!

guard were clubbed to death by their comrades for putting everyone's lives at risk.

If a whole unit fled from a battle they were '**decimated**'. 'Decimation' means 'removal of a tenth'. In other words, one in every ten soldiers was picked out and slaughtered!

Nevertheless, running away from the Roman army was pretty common, even though you risked such a terrible fate if you did it.

GROSS MOUSTACHES

But all the practice and ferocious discipline paid off. The Roman army marched all over Europe and successfully conquered tribe after tribe, and country after country.

One of its most successful generals was Julius Caesar. He was given the job of defeating the Gauls of northern France. The Romans called this area 'Gallia Comata', which means **Hairy Gaul** – because the tribes who lived there wore their hair long and had big moustaches.

The Romans couldn't stand moustaches. They thought they were unhygienic. They said that when the Gauls ate their meat, half of it got stuck and dangled in their face-hair, and when they drank, the booze ran through it like a sieve!

The tribes of Gaul had united under one leader called Vercingetorix. Gauls had crazy names to match their crazy moustaches.

Caesar's army pursued Vercingetorix and his men all over Gaul and eventually cornered them at a place called Alesia. The Gauls were inside Alesia looking out, and the Romans were outside looking in.

The French are still pretty proud of Vercingetorix – Napoleon put up this seven-metre-tall statue of him.
Why were they called the hairy Gauls?
I'd have thought that was obvious!

Caesar decided to wait the Gauls out – he figured it was only a matter of time before they ran out of food and were forced to eat their own moustaches. In the meantime, to be sure no more supplies got in and to keep his soldiers busy, he ordered a **huge wooden wall** be built around the town. The wall had . . .

. . . sharpened stakes at the top to stop people climbing over . . .

PLUS towers all along it . . .

PLUS three big trenches over 4 metres deep . . .

Caesar's soldiers were **so** brilliant at lifting, carrying and building that within a few weeks the wall was 10 miles long and 4 metres high.

PLUS loads of little pits filled with wooden stakes and covered with leaves and twigs (for the enemy to fall into).

PLUS another trench filled with water . . .

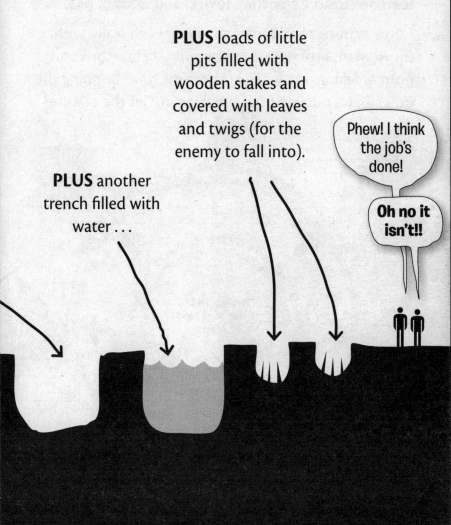

Then Caesar heard that 100,000 more Gauls were on their way to help rescue Vercingetorix's men. So he ordered his army to build **another** wall to protect them from the approaching Gauls. This second wall was even longer, running 14 miles round his men ... **PLUS** there were more trenches, towers and loads of pits.

Fierce fighting soon broke out along both walls, with the Romans attempting to prevent Vercingetorix's army from breaking out, while at the same time stopping the other Gauls outside from breaking in. Get the picture?

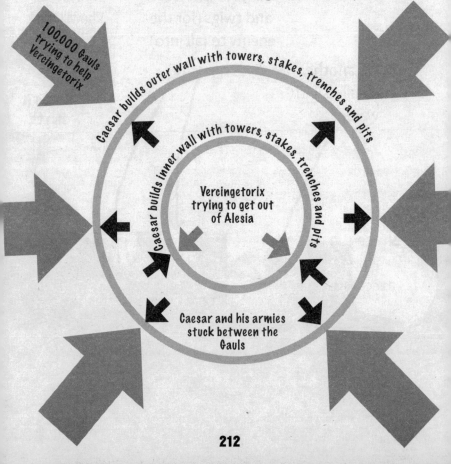

100,000 Gauls trying to help Vercingetorix

Caesar builds outer wall with towers, stakes, trenches and pits

Caesar builds inner wall with towers, stakes, trenches and pits

Vercingetorix trying to get out of Alesia

Caesar and his armies stuck between the Gauls

Despite being outnumbered 3 to 1, the Roman army defeated the attacking Gauls and prevented them from rescuing Vercingetorix's army. Vercingetorix and his men were forced to surrender or face starvation. The Gauls were beaten.

SIEGE OF ALESIA

Date: 52 BC

Roman Army: 60,000

Gauls: 80,000 inside the fort, plus another 100,000 outside!

Score: Romans –2, Gauls – 0

Man of the Match: Julius Caesar.

Vercingetorix was taken back to Rome in chains and was kept in prison for five years before being paraded through the streets as part of a big celebration of Caesar's military victories. After that, just to show everyone that no one should mess with the Romans, he was executed.

PEEWEE'S LIST OF ROMAN WEAPONS

The Roman army had some pretty nasty machines to help it fight people hidden behind giant walls. These included:

The '**Ballista**' – a large and powerful crossbow (like a bow and arrow but bigger and more complicated). It fired large iron-tipped bolts or darts that could punch through armour. Ballista bolts were said to be able to skewer several men at the same time!

The '**Onager**' – a giant catapult, which could be wound up and then released to fling massive chunks of rock at walls. 'Onager' means 'wild ass' because it kicked like a donkey!

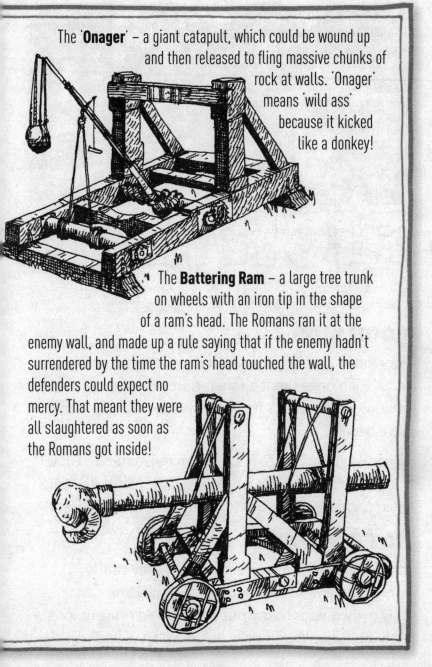

The **Battering Ram** – a large tree trunk on wheels with an iron tip in the shape of a ram's head. The Romans ran it at the enemy wall, and made up a rule saying that if the enemy hadn't surrendered by the time the ram's head touched the wall, the defenders could expect no mercy. That meant they were all slaughtered as soon as the Romans got inside!

POOR KIDS

Poor kids in ancient Rome lived in little flats and ate pizza. Rich ones spent all their time learning Latin and feasting on peacock's brains. Which would you rather have been?

Either way, you had to keep pretty quiet and do what you were told. Any kid who complained risked getting beaten, chucked out of the house or sold into slavery!

ROTTEN DADS

In ancient Rome, dads ruled. I mean they **really** ruled – they were the head of the family and not only owned your house but every single thing in it ... including you! You literally belonged to your dad, and

he was allowed to do whatever he wanted with you. When a baby was born, it was laid at its father's feet – if he picked it up it became part of the family, but if he didn't, it was abandoned.

Today if you misbehave, about the worst thing most parents will do to you is send you to your room. But in ancient Rome if you drove your dad nuts, he could take you miles away from home and abandon you in the street, or sell you as a slave to somebody else!

Until the first century AD, a father was even allowed to kill his children if he wanted!

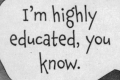

Someone liked this lad enough to carve his face. He did grow up to be Emperor Nero, mind.

I'm highly educated, you know.

It wouldn't have mattered if your mum wanted to keep you – mums didn't have much say in ancient Rome. They were expected to run the home, keep everything tidy, raise the children, cook nice food . . . and that was it.

Women belonged to their dad or their husband. For a long time they weren't even allowed to own things (everything in the house belonged to the head of the family), and they couldn't vote for changes to the law – so they just had to put up with things as they were, although I bet they worked out how to get their way when they wanted to!

DO I HAVE TO GO TO SCHOOL?

Lots of kids in ancient Rome didn't go to school – they were taught at home instead. Girls learned how to clean, sew and cook, while boys were taught whatever skills their dad thought they needed.

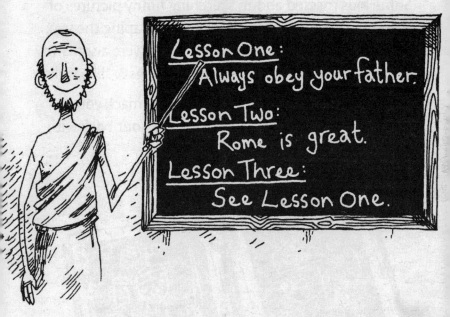

Lesson One:
Always obey your father.

Lesson Two:
Rome is great.

Lesson Three:
See Lesson One.

Most kids learned basic reading and writing and a bit of maths ... but not for long – from the age of ten, boys started working and girls got ready to get married!!

If you were from a rich family you had more of an education – you were sent to school till you were sixteen, were taught how to read and write in Latin and Greek, and how to speak in public.

Paper was rare and really expensive, so you practised writing by getting a pointed stick and scratching words on tablets covered in wax. If you wanted to erase something, you just smeared the wax back over the tablet and started again.

Some kids messed about, sketching funny pictures of their teachers on the wax tablets, or scraping the wax off it to make models. The sharp sticks were also handy for scratching your name on other things . . . like walls.

If you were caught, the teacher would smack your hands with a cane, or whip your back with strips of leather.

Roman teachers who did this a lot were given nicknames like 'leather arm' and 'the whacker'!

Teachers weren't paid very much. In fact, one complained that he got paid in a year what a chariot driver got paid for one race!

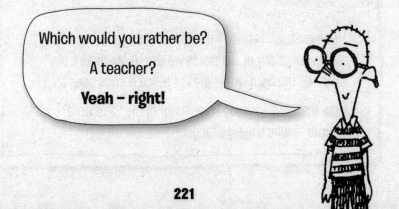

A **chariot driver** would get glamour, excitement, money – and possibly an early death.

A **teacher** would get pesky kids, loads of homework to mark – and a long, pleasant retirement in a villa by the sea.

Which would you rather be?

A teacher?

Yeah – right!

WAYS WITH WORDS

The language the Romans used was called Latin . . . Hang on a moment – here is a newsflash!

We **interrupt** this **chapter** to bring you a **special announcement**. **Scientists** have **discovered aliens**. They are a **strange type** of **animal** with **six tentacles**, and they've **promised** not to **eat** us if we send them **flowers**. **Florists** are **expected** to sell out of **roses** soon, which are **apparently** their **favourite**.

This newsflash (actually it's not real, did you realize that?) shows how many of the words we use today come from Latin. All the **bold** words are Latin, the normal ones aren't.

Even the word 'language' comes from the Latin word '**lingua**' – which means tongue!

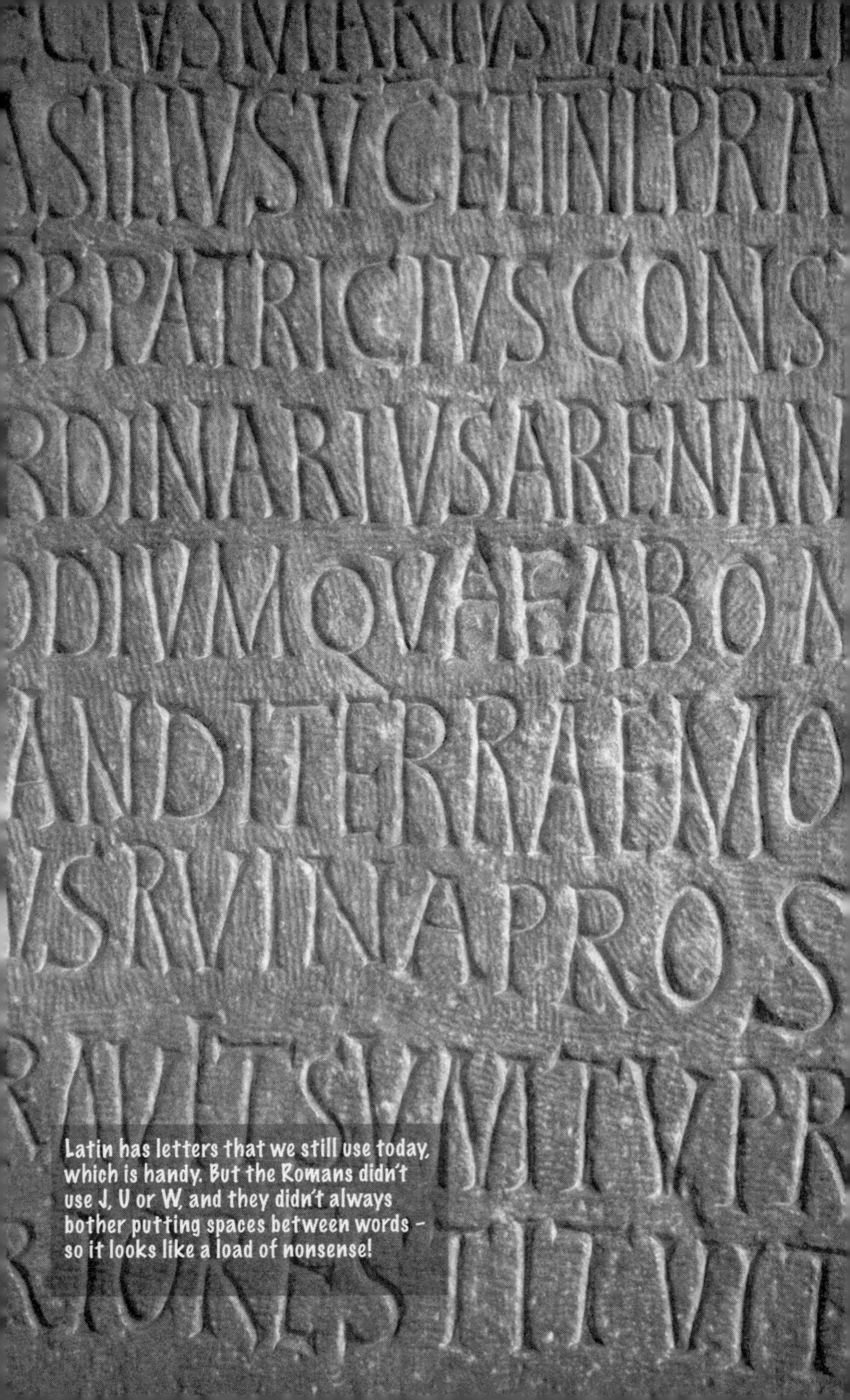

GIVSMARIVSVENA
SILVSVCHINPRA
RBPATRICIVSCONS
RDINARIVSARENAN
DIVMOVAEABOA
ANDITERRAEMO
VSRVINAPROS
RAVETSVVITVR
RIONES IIIVI

Latin has letters that we still use today, which is handy. But the Romans didn't use J, U or W, and they didn't always bother putting spaces between words – so it looks like a load of nonsense!

THE CURIOSITY CREW TEACHES YOU TO SPEAK THE LINGO

Here are some Latin phrases to impress your friends . . .

Te audire non possum est. Musa sapientum fixa est in aure.

I can't hear you. I have a banana in my ear.

Non torsii subligarium!

Don't get your knickers in a twist!

. . . Unfortunately they probably won't understand you, because not many people speak Latin any more.

MOUSE AND CART

When they weren't busy learning Latin and doing whatever their dads told them to, Roman kids played with toys, games and pets.

Most of their toys sound a bit lame to us – things like balls, spinning tops, hoops, toy soldiers and dolls made of clay or wax.

But there are also descriptions of Roman kids fighting mock battles with wooden swords, and playing tug-of-war games where one team had to try and pull another team across a line.

This way ...

Lots of children kept pet birds – doves, ducks, crows and geese were popular – and if you were lucky you might even own a pet monkey! Some kids had dogs which they hooked up to mini-chariots, then raced them round the streets. Others made little carts for mice to pull.

Who needs a Wii when you've got a mouse pulling a tiny cart!

AND NOW THE RICH KIDS

Rich kids lived in big villas. They had kitchens, dining rooms, baths, a garden and everyone had their own bedroom. You might even have had a villa near the city **and** a seaside home for the summer.

JOJO'S GUIDE TO RICH KIDS' HOUSES

A rich kid's luxury villa was kitted out with ancient state-of-the-art technology . . .

Central heating: The Romans designed a way to keep their feet toasty warm, because their villas had stone floors which got chilly in winter. Spaces under the floor called hypocausts were filled with hot air heated by a furnace.

Glass windows: Glass was a new invention and mostly used for making small things like bottles and cups. But some rich Romans had little glass windows – although they couldn't see much through them because the glass was bluey-green with bubbles in it!

HEAT

Baths: Lots of villas had their own bath-houses with steam rooms (heated by the hypocaust) and ice-cold plunge baths.

Swanky decorations: The floors and walls were often decorated with mosaics – pictures made up of thousands of tiny pieces of coloured stone (even simple mosaics had around 100,000 pieces, some smaller than your fingernail). You could choose the picture you wanted from a book or design your own, then someone would come and fit it all together. A bit like doing the world's biggest jigsaw puzzle!

BAKED DORMICE

Romans loved their food. If you lived in a small flat which didn't have a kitchen, your mum or dad would get takeaways from fast food shops – things like bread soaked in wine, sausages, and pizzas (although they didn't look like today's pizzas – tomatoes weren't grown in Europe until hundreds of years later!).

But if you were rich, your mum and dad would show off by having massive dinner parties that lasted hours – one emperor served a meal of 22 courses. At these parties they would eat really extravagant dishes – the weirder the better!

And their favourite was stinky fish sauce. It was called '**garum**', and made of rotten fish guts. Boy, did it smell! But it was really popular and the Romans put it on everything, just like we splurge our grub with ketchup! Garum factories were often located far outside towns – I can't think why!!

For big feasts, cooks would stuff one animal inside another – maybe a chicken stuffed inside a duck stuffed inside a goose stuffed inside a pig stuffed inside a cow! It must have felt like you were eating an entire farm!

And they made joke food too; things like roast hare with wings attached to it, to make it look like a big flying rabbit!

SLAVE KIDS

Slavery was very common in Roman times. If you were rich, you had lots of slaves to do things for you. On the other hand, if you were a foreign child who'd been captured by the Romans, you had to spend your whole life being somebody else's slave . . . great, huh?

Slaves were sold at public auctions in marketplaces – they had to stand with a scroll around their neck which described their name, their nationality, and what they looked like. Slave dealers had to guarantee the slaves they sold were free from disease and wouldn't steal anything or run away. If there was something wrong with them, like they were really sick or they'd tried to commit suicide because they were so lonely, they could be returned and the owners got their money back.

A rich man could own 500 slaves and an Emperor might have more than **20,000!**

Having slaves was great – slaves would . . .

- carry your books to school
- clean your room
- cook your food
- wash your clothes

. . . and they could be made to do this over and over again without you having to pay them any money.

Being a slave wasn't so great. If you were lucky you might work for a nice family who looked after you and gave you decent food to eat. If not you'd be overworked and underfed, and you'd get beaten if you complained about it.

Unskilled slaves were sent to work on big farms, sweating in the fields all day in the hot sun or doing hard, horrible work underground in mines.

PULL!

Roman traders even had slave-powered ships, rowed by slaves who were chained to the oars.

Slaves often had their faces branded with a mark (by burning them with hot metal) or wore collars like dogs so that people would know who they belonged to.

Even if your master died, you weren't freed – you were just passed on to somebody else. The only way to stop being a slave was if you were set free by your master, or if you saved enough money to buy your freedom. This was pretty difficult, though, because slaves weren't paid anything.

FVGITENEME
CVMREVOCV
VERIS ME·DM
ONINOACCIPIS
SOLIDVM

This collar was found in Rome.

THE SONS OF MARS

PART THREE

While he was in Gaul, Julius Caesar (that moustache-hating army general you met on page 208) led a couple of expeditions across the English Channel to take a look at a strange island known as 'Britannia'.

BLUE BANDY BRITONS

He told the Romans that the Britons wore their hair long and shaved every part of their body except their heads and upper lips – more moustaches! And before battle, they used a natural dye to paint themselves blue, which made them look pretty scary in a fight.

But as they had lots of cattle and precious metals, he thought the Britons were probably worth conquering, although not by him, as he'd got more important things to do.

Like the Gauls, the Britons were divided into lots of different tribes. Some of them wanted to be friends with Rome, but others thought Rome was a very bad thing indeed.

Eventually, in 43 AD, the Romans finally invaded. Some tribes welcomed them with open arms, while others cracked open the blue paint and got busy sharpening their battle swords!

The Romans successfully conquered most of the tribes in the south and east, and Britannia became part of the **Roman Empire**. There was just one problem – there were quite a lot of tribes which still hadn't been beaten, and they weren't going to go down without a fight . . .

BRITISH TRIBES WHEN THE ROMANS ARRIVED

Brigantes

Parisi

Deceangli

Ordivices

Coritani

Iceni

Cornovii

Catevellauni

Demetae

Silures

Trinovantes

Dobunni

Atrebates

Cantiaci

Belgae

Regnenses

Durotriges

Dumnonii

BOUDICCAN REVOLT

One of the tribes which hadn't yet been conquered was called the Iceni (pronounced *I-see-nee*). They'd done a deal with the Romans, which allowed them to remain free as long as they paid 'tribute' (which meant giving Rome lots of presents).

But when their King died in 60 AD, the Roman Emperor said the land of the Iceni must now be handed over to Rome. And if the Iceni didn't like it – tough nuts! So who was going to stand up for the Iceni?

Come on, if you think you're hard enough!

A statue of Boudicca in London. Nice wheels!

The answer was **Boudicca** (pronounced *Boo-dik-ah*), the wife of the former king. She raised an army and marched south to attack the Roman base at Colchester. Other tribes, who also hated Rome, joined in and the revolt spread.

After seizing Colchester, Boudicca's army attacked the new Roman towns of London and St Albans. Today if you dig deep into the ground in these cities you'll find a layer of black and red ash – this is the remains of the buildings Boudicca's army destroyed!

You might be asking – what were the Romans doing while all this was going on? Well, their legions had been busy fighting tribes in Wales – and as soon as they heard what Boudicca was up to, they rushed back.

The two armies finally met on a Roman road called Watling Street. The Romans were outnumbered 10 to 1 and stood facing hundreds of thousands of wild screaming Britons with painted faces – men and women – clashing their weapons, blowing trumpets and thumping drums.

But if you think this made the Romans nervous – think again. This was the Roman army remember . . . and the Roman army knew their way around a battlefield.

Fight! Fight!

HOW TO FIGHT LIKE A TORTOISE

The Roman army was trained to fight in close formation – thousands of soldiers could march forward or back, and turn left or right, without bumping into one another. Each man's shield overlapped the next to make a wall of shields, with the pilums (big sticks) and spears sticking out in front.

One famous formation was the '**testudo**' or 'tortoise'. Men stood in a square with shields round the sides and over their heads to form a protective shell. These shields were so strongly interlinked that it was said you could drive a horse and chariot over the top!

RRAAARGH!!

Another formation was called the 'wedge'; legionaries formed up in a triangle, then the blokes at the front charged forward, with their swords driving the enemy line apart.

Most importantly, the Roman army always formed up carefully, quickly and in **total** silence! This took incredible discipline and would've been very off-putting for the enemy – it's a bit scary to see that the army you're about to fight is quietly getting ready to obliterate you.

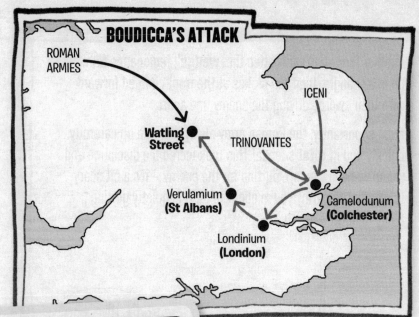

BOUDICCA'S ATTACK

ROMAN ARMIES

ICENI

Watling Street

TRINOVANTES

Verulamium (St Albans)

Camelodunum (Colchester)

Londinium (London)

BATTLE OF WATLING STREET

Date: 61 AD approx.

Roman Army: 10,000

Britons: 100,000+

Score: Romans – 1, Britons – 1 (Rome wins on penalties after extra time)

Wo-Man of the match: Queen Boudicca (10/10 for effort, 1/10 for technique)

Riding in a chariot, Boudicca led her troops in a charge against the Roman legionaries. Unfortunately it was like running into a wall (a wall with sharp spikes sticking out of it). The British tribes retreated in confusion and chaos. The Romans marched on, slaughtering everyone in their path.

By the end, only 400 Romans had died and 80,000 Britons had been killed! It was a massacre (or 'a glorious victory' if you were a Roman).

A SCOTTISH MUG

The Romans went on to defeat a lot of the other British tribes but they never succeeded in taking the whole island. They gave up when they reached Scotland, and built a big stone wall across the whole of northern England to mark the border of the Empire.

It was called 'Hadrian's Wall' because it was built during the rule of the Roman Emperor Hadrian. It took the army eight years to put it up, and it had forts and towers positioned all along it so the army could keep an eye on the barbarians beyond.

CALEDONIA (Scotland)

BRITANNIA (Britain)

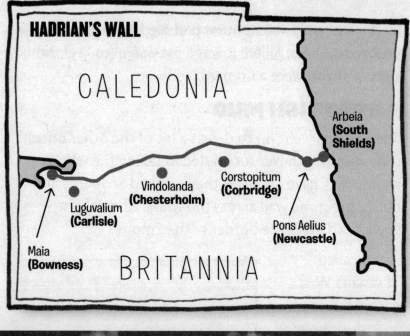

HADRIAN'S WALL

CALEDONIA

Arbeia
(South
Shields)

Vindolanda
(Chesterholm)

Corstopitum
(Corbridge)

Luguvalium
(Carlisle)

Pons Aelius
(Newcastle)

Maia
(Bowness)

BRITANNIA

There are still long unbroken stretches of Hadrian's Wall you can walk along today.

Hadrian's Wall was so impressive that the Romans made souvenir mugs with pictures of the wall on them and the names of the forts round the rim!

The remains of Hadrian's Wall and its forts are still standing, so you can go and see it for yourself – and maybe get your own mug while you're there.

LITTLE BRITONS

One of the forts near Hadrian's Wall was called 'Vindolanda' (look at the map opposite) and in the 1970s a load of Roman wooden writing tablets were found there preserved in an ancient rubbish dump. They include fragments of letters from soldiers stationed on the wall, including birthday invitations and requests for more beer! They tell us that the soldiers called the local tribes 'The Brittunculi' or 'Little Britons' and that they missed the warm weather of home. One letter is a reply to a soldier who'd asked for more underpants!

Vindolanda fort has been recreated for visitors.

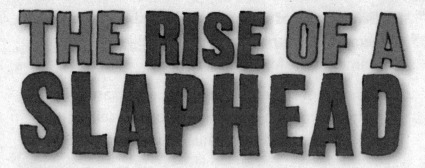

THE RISE OF A SLAPHEAD

For a long time, the Roman Republic was really successful – power was shared between the Senate and the people of Rome, and although there were lots of rows and the occasional uprising, by and large it was working out OK. But then things started to go wrong . . .

I've lost my job.

Yeah, those selfish slaves are doing all the work for free.

Someone nicked my farm when I was away fighting in the army.

Meanwhile rich Roman politicians were pocketing bribes and fixing prices to make sure they got even richer.

And then everyone started fighting over how Rome should be run. Things looked bad.

The men perfectly placed to take advantage of this aggravation were the generals of the Roman army – experienced leaders with thousands of men at their command.

And which general reckoned he could rule Rome better than anyone else?

Who'd launched the first expedition to Britannia?

Who'd smashed the hairy Gauls?

Who was a national hero?

Cool it, guys. I'm in charge now!

Hooray!!

Yes, you've guessed . . . **Julius Caesar**.

He marched back home with a legion of soldiers and made himself 'dictator' of Rome.

Being dictator meant that everyone had to do what he said. In the past 'dictators' had been appointed at times of crisis, but only for six months, after which they'd handed control back to the people.

But Caesar had no intention of handing over to somebody else – ever; oh no . . . he made himself dictator for life!

Statues of Caesar dressed like a god were put up and his face was stamped on Roman coins so everyone knew who was in charge. But he was very vain. On the coins he insisted on wearing a crown of leaves round his forehead to cover his big shiny bald head.

Baldy, aka Julius Caesar, wearing his wig.

Caesar won the support of ordinary Romans by spending lots of money on public games and banquets, cancelling debts and doing massive makeovers on the big public buildings in Rome.

Unfortunately for him, he didn't win everybody over. Some people thought he was too powerful. In 44 BC Caesar was assassinated – stabbed on the steps of Senate House. The men who killed him believed they were freeing Rome from tyranny and restoring power to the people – hurrah!

Unfortunately that was utter rubbish. All that happened was another lot of generals started fighting over who should take Caesar's place – boo!

The man who's just killed Caesar is saying what a nice chap Caesar was and what a shame it is he's dead . . .

NEVER IGNORE A CHICKEN

Nowadays most people who want to have a chat with their god pop down to their local place of worship and do a bit of praying. But not the Romans. Their religion made them do some seriously crazy things, like sticking their hands in animal guts and looking for hidden messages, chopping the heads off dead bodies, and running around dressed in goat skins whipping people!

Sometimes this was just a way of having a wild time, but mostly they did it because they thought it would keep the gods happy. They had lots and lots of gods, and they didn't want to make any of them angry. It's easy to understand why – the gods were . . .

THE FAMILY FROM HELL!!!

Mmm . . . tasty.

Saturn was the grand-daddy of the gods. He tried to eat all his children so they wouldn't take over from him.

Jupiter was the son of Saturn – one of the few of his children who managed to avoid being eaten. He fought his dad and became king of the gods. He had a thunderbolt which he threw at anyone he didn't like.

Neptune was Jupiter's brother and the god of the sea. When he was feeling grouchy and bad-tempered he stirred up the ocean and wrecked ships.

Juno was Jupiter's wife, and queen of the gods. She spent a lot of time arguing with her husband, bossing him about or flirting with him to get her way.

Are you, looking for a fight?

Mars was the son of Jupiter, the god of war and the dad of Romulus and Remus. He was a thug who loved nothing more than a good bloody battle. The Romans thought he was great!

Mercury was the son of Jupiter. He could move around really fast and was a thief and a trickster. He tried to steal Jupiter's thunderbolt but burned his fingers!

Venus was the goddess of love and beauty. She was the girlfriend of Mars, but often pranced around without any clothes on and got off with loads of other blokes. She was always poking her nose into other people's love-lives.

TOO NUDE FOR KIDS!

Imagine having that lot living next door!

SPOT THE GOD

The Romans believed the gods were everywhere. Apart from Saturn and Mars and their family, they thought there were gods in the trees, stones, lakes, caves and flowers, as well as in things like stoves and beds. They even thought there was a little god who lived in the latch that opened the door to your house!

So how did the Roman worshippers keep all these squabbling gods happy?

By doing exactly the same thing that makes you and me happy . . . they gave them presents!

Not iPhones and trainers. Usually they handed over things like food, money or flowers. But on special occasions they presented the gods with their favourite present of all . . . the **blood and guts** of a really big animal!

VEGETARIANS SHOULD NOT READ THIS NEXT BIT AS IT'S RATHER DISGUSTING!

GRACE'S NOTES ON HOW THE ROMANS SACRIFICED A BIG ANIMAL

1 They took the biggest and best cow, pig or sheep they could find.

Who me?

2 They scrubbed it up until it looked really cute, and decorated it with pretty ribbons.

256

3 Then they led it to the temple, and handed it over to the priest.

OINK . . . OOIIINNK!

CENSORED!

4 The priest cut its throat, drained it blood, removed its insides and burned them on an altar.

5 The priest's helpers cooked the animal on a barbecue and served it up to everyone with lots of wine.

Sometimes over a **hundred** animals were sacrificed at one time. This was pretty messy, though, and meant all the worshippers ended up with bursting bellies, grease round their mouths and sticky fingers!

WHAT DOES IT ALL MEAN?

Romans were always looking for signs to tell them whether the gods were happy or angry. These were known as 'omens'. If you saw a bad omen, it meant the gods were upset and the safest thing to do was go home, lock the door and hide under the bed.

Help! It's the end of the world . . .

If a black cat entered your house, it was an awful omen. So was a cock crowing during a banquet. If you spilt wine or oil, or tripped over your doorstep, big trouble was coming.

If I was a Roman I'd never have left my house!

Before anything important was done in Rome – like passing a law or going to war – professional omen-readers were brought in to find out what the gods thought. They looked for omens in lots of things. For instance . . .

The weather: When a storm blew up and thunder and lightning kicked off, they listened to it to try and work out what the gods were saying.

Animal guts: A priest would cut open the belly of an animal to see if there were any signs from the gods in the shape and colour of its guts.

That doesn't look good . . .

Bird song: They watched birds flapping about, and listened to them chirruping, because they believed that the birds were transmitting coded messages from the god Jupiter.

LISTEN TO THAT CHICKEN

The Roman army swore by omens too. They took sacred chickens with them into battle, and before attacking they'd choose one and crumble some food in front of it. If the chicken ate the food, it was a good omen; if it didn't, the omen was most definitely **BAD**.

In 249 BC before a sea battle, a sacred chicken refused to eat and the commander threw it overboard – saying if it couldn't eat, then at least it could drink! Of course, he lost the battle – which proves you should always listen to a sacred chicken!

I'm simply NOT hungry.

A SERIOUSLY BAD OMEN

In the year 114 BC, there was a really bad sign. A sacred priestess at one of the temples in Rome was struck by lightning . . . GASP!

People thought the temple priestesses had seriously annoyed the gods by having boyfriends, which was the worst thing a priestess could do.

There was only one way to make the gods happy again – sacrifice some humans!

So they took two Greeks and two Gauls and buried them alive under the marketplace. Now you probably think that this was not only incredibly cruel, but also incredibly stupid. But the Romans reckoned it worked, because after that not one single priestess was struck by lightning again.

MONSTERS

Ancient Romans also believed in monsters, including:

● **witches** who could change into birds

● men who became **wolves** when it grew dark

● and a serpent-tailed **demon** called 'Lamia' who stalked the shadows looking for children to eat.

It's a wonder anyone could sleep at night.

And if that's not creepy enough, they also believed in ghosts called 'lemures'. They said that if you didn't give dead people a proper burial, they would come back as lemures and haunt you. To stop that from happening, they chopped the heads off the dead, and put heavy stones on their coffins. The lemures can't have been all that creepy, though, because if you had a 'lemures' problem, all you had to do to scare them away was bang your cooking pots!

Don't hit the pots too hard: they're made of clay!

BURIED WITH RUBBISH

The dead weren't allowed to be buried inside the walls of a city, so the roads leading out were always lined with burials. This meant that people who wanted to go to a funeral had to go on a big hike.

The Romans loved a nice funeral. If you died, you were given a good wash and laid on a couch in your nicest clothes for eight days. Then there'd be a big procession. If you weren't very popular your relations would hire some professional mourners who'd make a big fuss over you and make it look like everyone missed you!

Your body was either put straight in a stone tomb or else it was burned on a big bonfire, after which your ashes were tipped into a pot and then placed in the tomb.

Wail, wail, even more wailing . . .

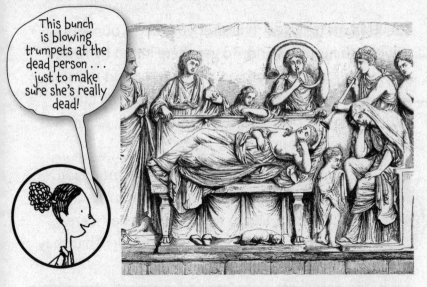

Every Roman wanted a nice funeral; even slaves would put together the few pennies they had saved up to pay for one. They knew that if they couldn't raise the cash, they'd get no funeral at all. Instead their body would be dumped in a pit on the outskirts of town at a grim place called 'Potter's Field', along with the local rubbish, dead animals and the scrapings off the road.

The Romans believed that after you died, your soul went to the underworld. To get there it had be rowed across the River of Death on a little ferry, and to make sure the ghostly ferryman did his job properly and didn't lose your body or mess about with it, a coin was placed in your mouth to pay him.

 Some Romans believed that the more you paid, the better your journey across the River of Death would be, so they were buried with their jewels, in order that they could travel first class!

Charon the ferryman arrives to take the dead across the River Styx.

Fares, please!

CHRISTIANS FOR LUNCH

Christianity started when the Romans crucified Jesus Christ in about 30 AD. They thought he was a dangerous troublemaker who'd disrespected their gods. They didn't think much of his followers either, because Christians only believed in one God and refused to worship any of the others – not even those little ones living in your door latches.

The Romans believed the Christians were putting Rome in danger by not worshipping Mars (the god of war, remember?) and the rest of his family. They thought the gods would get cross about this and bad things would happen. So they started rounding up the Christians and killing them in all sorts of horrible ways, including feeding them to lions!

Despite this, Christianity spread right across the Empire. People were simply impressed by all these brave Christians who'd rather die than give up their religion!

Early Christians couldn't shout about their faith, so they used a fish symbol (drawn in the dirt or on a wall) to let other believers know they were Christians.

ROME'S CRAZIEST EMPERORS

After Julius Caesar was assassinated there was a long civil war, at the end of which his nephew Octavian became ruler of Rome. He was the first person to call himself 'Emperor', which meant 'Supreme Commander', and he changed his name to Augustus, which meant 'the Great One'. He certainly wasn't shy, was he?

From then on, around 27 BC, Rome was no longer a Republic, it was officially an 'Empire' and it carried on being one for hundreds of years.

There were about 140 Roman Emperors in total. They were the most powerful men in Rome, with oodles of money and an army at their command. If you lived in the Empire you had to do whatever the Emperor said.

When an Emperor died, the new Emperor was often one of his relatives, even if they weren't the best person for the job.

Some Emperors were good, some were bad and some were just plain **crazy** – I'm talking about the most demented, unhinged, half-baked, 'mad as a box of frogs', 'one-way ticket to the loony bin' freaks ever to put on a toga . . .

This would have been funny if they hadn't had the power of life and death over everyone in the Roman Empire.

Caligula (reigned 37-41 AD)

Another early Roman Emperor was Caligula. A few months after taking power, he came down with a strange illness, which seems to have turned him into a total nutter. He proclaimed himself a god and built a temple with a life-size gold statue of himself inside it. He raised taxes so he could roll around on piles of gold coins, and held lavish banquets where he drank pearls dissolved in vinegar. He even made his pet horse a senator and built him a big marble stable to live in!

Caligula was a fan of violence and torture – once at a sporting event he ordered the first five rows of the audience to be thrown to the lions because he was bored. His favourite method of torture was hanging people upside down and sawing them in half.

Oi, Senator Dobbin – stop eating your toga!

Nero (reigned 54–68 AD)

Nero was a big show-off. He took part in chariot races where he made sure he was crowned the winner even if he lost. He also put on shows where people were forced to sit and listen to him acting and singing for hours and hours. Some of the audience even pretended to be dead so they'd be carried out!

> Don't stop me if you've heard this one before.

He thought everyone was plotting against him (which they probably were) so he got rid of anyone he didn't trust – including his own mother. He poisoned her (but she took an antidote), crushed her bed with a collapsible ceiling (but she escaped) and sabotaged a boat so that it would sink when she was on it (she survived and swam ashore). Finally he sent three assassins to stab her to death and then pretended it was suicide. That one worked!

PURPLE PEOPLE

Roman Emperors often wore special purple robes – purple dye was very rare and expensive: only the rich could afford it. It came from a type of sea snail and you had to crush up thousands of them to get even a few drops of dye. The colour became known as 'imperial purple' and it was forbidden for anyone else in Rome to wear that colour. The sale of purple was even punishable by death!

Commodus (reigned 177-192 AD)

The Emperor Commodus loved pretending to be a gladiator (a kind of professional wrestler), although his fights weren't always fair, particularly when he decided to take on people with no arms or legs. In fact sometimes he tied them up beforehand – he wasn't taking any chances, was he? He also loved fighting exotic animals – he boasted that he'd slaughtered 100 lions in a single day, killed three elephants single-handedly and shot the head off an ostrich.

If you were an insane Roman Emperor you had to watch out – there were always people plotting to get rid of you. Even good Emperors often came to a sticky end – knocked off by relatives, politicians or even their own bodyguards! No wonder they were paranoid.

FUN STUFF

If you were a smart Emperor you'd spend loads of money putting on free entertainment for the ordinary people, because this made you really popular!

Plus, if everyone was busy watching sport, they might not notice when you did something really unpopular like raising taxes.

CHARIOT RACING

A Roman writer once said that there were only two things that ordinary Romans were interested in – cheap food and 'circuses'.

He didn't mean circuses with clowns, acrobats and tightrope walkers.

A 'circus' was the Roman name for a stadium that put on chariot races.

Chariot racing was Rome's most popular sport – just like football is today. And the 'Circus Maximus' was Rome's Wembley Stadium. In fact it was bigger! It could hold up to 250,000 people – more than double the number of people who can fit into Wembley – and entry was free!

El Djem in Tunisia held 35,000 spectators for chariot racing or gladiator fights.

Charioteers were divided into teams – the blues, the greens, the whites and the reds – and they all wore their team colours. Fans followed their favourite team and knew all about the different horses and drivers. The best drivers were treated like Premiership footballers – they earned loads of money and had their pictures put on things like cups, sculptures and mosaics.

Some Romans would do anything for their team – at the funeral of one Red driver, a Red supporter threw himself on the funeral bonfire along with the body . . . and you thought football fans were crazy!

The Romans were so obsessed with chariot racing, they even put pictures of it on their coins.

At the start of each race, the chariots lined up in front of gates. When they were all ready, a cloth was dropped on the floor to signal the start. The gates sprang open and the teams of horses thundered on to the track.

On your marks, get set, giddy up!

Chariots were usually pulled by four horses, and the driver would wrap the reins around him to help steer. Competitors would deliberately try to make their opponents crash. If a chariot turned over, the driver was dragged around the track and often trampled to death.

Not surprisingly, a chariot driver wasn't expected to live long – one celebrity driver called Scorpus won over 2,000 races before being killed in a crash when he was only twenty-seven years old.

GLADIATORS

The only thing more dangerous than being a charioteer was being a gladiator – a trained fighter who risked his life in front of sell-out crowds.

The Colosseum in Rome was a massive four-storey stone arena with tiered seats for 50,000 spectators. The word 'arena' means 'sandy place' because the floor was covered in sand to soak up all the blood. And the best seats were at the front, close to the action. If you were lucky you might even get splatted with gore!

The remains of the Colosseum are still standing in Rome today.

Lots of different shows were put on at the Colosseum – animal fights, hunts, public executions and battle re-enactments – but the most popular were the gladiator fights. Men, women and children flocked to watch these contests . . . it was a fun day out for all the family.

The name 'gladiator' comes from the Roman word 'gladius' or sword. Armed with swords, spears and daggers, they fought each other or ferocious wild animals like lions and tigers (who'd often been starved for days so they were extra hungry and grouchy). It was often a fight to the death – the winner was the last man (or lion) left alive.

Roman animal collectors went all round the Empire gathering up exotic beasts to put in their gladiator shows – leopards, lions, tigers, elephants and bears. So many were killed that whole species almost became extinct!

The bloke in the big hat isn't trying to look up the skirt of the one with the giant fork. He's stabbing him in the leg.

The gladiators had as little choice as the animals – most were slaves, criminals or prisoners-of-war taken captive and forced to become gladiators. If they refused to fight they were executed. If they were good enough, they might win fame and fortune – and eventually maybe even their freedom.

Some free men also signed up because of the glory and the prize money . . . and because they were nutters.

They trained at special 'gladiator schools' where they practised fighting with different weapons. Gladiators were difficult to replace, so while they were alive they were well looked after, with lots of food to eat and doctors on hand to treat their injuries.

I can't see a thing in this ridiculous helmet . . . now where did that lion go?

JOJO'S FAVOURITE GLADIATORS

I'm really hard.

Retiarii ('net fighters') – carried a trident, a dagger and a net to entangle their opponents.

Sagittarii ('archers') – mounted on horses and armed with a bow and arrow.

I'm harder.

Thraces ('Thracian soldiers') – armed with a small shield, a wide-brimmed helmet and a curved sword.

I'm harder than the lot of you.

Andabatae (horseback fighters) – dressed in chainmail, wore helmets without eyeholes (!) and charged blindly around the arena.

Essedarii (war charioteers) – named after the chariots the Celts rode into battle.

I'm the hardest!

Bestiarii (animal fighters) – armed with spears or knives, they fought exotic imported beasts.

But it wasn't just fully grown men who fought. There are descriptions of women and dwarf gladiators.

The fights were part of spectacular shows with music, props and scenery (just like going to the theatre but with more severed limbs). Under the floor of the Colosseum were underground chambers and tunnels. Slaves pulling on ropes could hoist scenery or animals up through trapdoors into the centre of the arena. If you wanted to stage a sea battle, the whole place could even be flooded with water from the nearby aqueduct!

Gladiator fights often had referees. They were probably needed to make sure the fight was fair and to call half-time – even ferocious gladiators needed a bit of a rest now and again.

Once a gladiator had floored his opponent, it was up to the crowd (or the Emperor if he was watching) to decide whether the loser was to be killed or spared. Sometimes if both men had fought well, they were both allowed to live to fight another day.

Crowds showed they wanted the loser to die by with a 'pollice verso' – Latin for 'turned thumb'. But did that mean thumbs up, or down? No one knows!

SPARTACUS

Some Romans worried about the use of gladiators. They thought putting lots of slaves, criminals and ex-soldiers together, teaching them how to kill and giving them weapons might lead to trouble. And guess what . . . they were right!

In 73 BC, seventy gladiators led by an ex-soldier called Spartacus, broke out of a Gladiator School in southern Italy, seizing weapons and armour on the way out. They raided the surrounding countryside and recruited other slaves to join their revolt.

They knew it wouldn't be long before the army would be sent to sort them out, so they made their way up to the top of the volcano Mount Vesuvius. This wasn't such a daft idea as it sounds: the volcano was dormant – meaning it was safe to climb – and from the top they could see anyone coming to get them.

> We demand our freedom – and some trousers.

Three thousand Roman soldiers were sent to deal with the gladiators. They camped out at the bottom of the volcano and waited for them to starve. But Spartacus and his men weaved ropes out of vines and abseiled down the cliffs on the other side, then launched a surprise attack on the camp, killing the soldiers and stealing their kit.

It was clearly going to take a whole lot more to stop Spartacus – so next Rome sent two whole legions (10,000 strong) to wipe out the slaves. But even that wasn't enough to stop them! By now lots of slaves across Italy had heard what was going on and joined the revolt – Spartacus soon had a force of over 70,000 men!!

Now people back in Rome got really panicky – there were a lot of slaves in Rome: what if they all started rising up? Who'd be left to do all the rubbish jobs like scraping dead skin off the floor of the baths or washing togas in vats of urine?

This time, eight legions were sent to put down the revolt and the slave army was finally destroyed.

We don't know what happened to Spartacus – he might have been killed in battle, or maybe he was one of 6,000 defeated slaves crucified afterwards along the Appian Way – the main road into Rome.

Rome wanted to make it very, very clear to every slave that they mustn't ever do anything like that ever again. Do you have a funny feeling that the Romans were getting a bit scared?

THE EMPIRE FALLS APART

At first Emperors tended to survive for quite a long while, even if they were barking mad like Nero and Caligula, but people got fed up with all this scary behaviour and tried to put a stop to it. Soon Emperors were lucky if they lasted more than a couple of years before getting poisoned, stabbed, having their heads chopped off, being pushed down the stairs or suffocating to death with their own underpants (OK, as far as I know, no Roman Emperor was actually suffocated to death with his own underpants... but I'm sure somebody thought about doing it).

Some Emperors only lasted a few weeks before they were bumped off!

But while everyone in Rome was busy scheming and plotting and knocking off Emperors... the Empire was falling apart.

WATCH YOUR BACK

Often Emperors ended up being killed by the men paid to protect them ... their own bodyguards!

The Praetorian Guard was a unit of elite soldiers whose job was to look after the Emperor and keep order in the city of Rome – a bit like a police force.

But if you paid them enough money they might switch sides and assassinate the Emperor for you ... handy. Sometimes they got fed up with the Emperor and, just for the fun of it, killed him and replaced him with somebody else.

Once they even held an auction and sold the job of Emperor to the highest bidder!

I think I should have stayed at home.

When Emperor Galbus didn't pay the Praetorian Guards, they rioted ... and killed him!

291

TOO BIG FOR ITS BOOTS

The land the Romans ruled over was now absolutely ginormous – it had swollen from a tiny bunch of villages to an Empire bigger than even cocky Romulus could ever have dreamed of – 2.2 million square miles, to be precise, with a whopping 120 million people living in it.

Lots of the places you might visit on holiday – like France, Spain, Italy, Germany, Greece, Turkey and Egypt – were all once part of the Roman Empire. The Romans built towns in all these places and the people who lived there started calling themselves 'Romans', speaking Latin and wearing trendy togas.

ALL ROADS LEAD TO ROME

To help people get round their colossal Empire, what did the Romans build? Well, if you know nothing else at all about the Romans, you probably know that they built roads . . . lots of them . . . over 53,000 miles of them . . . by hand! . . . and most of them were dead straight!

So you're probably thinking: roads aren't anything special. They're just big, dark grey things that graze my knee when I fall off my bike. But in the past if you wanted to get anywhere you had to trudge along little winding tracks, sinking up to your knees in mud whenever it rained. Now everyone could travel in style along wide stone roads that linked up all the places in the Empire.

Roman roads were made as straight as possible to make the journey quicker but they weren't always **totally** straight – the Romans weren't stupid: if there was a big mountain in the way, they went around it!

A Roman road around the Gredos Mountains in Spain.

The Appian Way in Rome. This was one of the first important Roman roads ever built. When it was finished, it connected Rome in the north to Brindisi all the way down in the south, 350 miles away.

A PROBLEM HALVED

The trouble was, as the Empire got bigger and bigger, it got harder and harder to run – there just weren't enough soldiers or money to keep it all going. In fact it got so bloomin' massive no one could hold it together.

In 284 AD the Emperor Diocletian tried to make things easier by cutting the Empire in two – a Western Empire and an Eastern Empire, each with its own ruler.

Unfortunately, it would have taken more than a pair of scissors to solve all Rome's problems.

A DIVIDED EMPIRE

How do you divide the Roman Empire?

Use a pair of Caesars!

Eastern Empire

Western Empire

I'M BORED!

Slaves did all the work in ancient Rome. They slaved away in factories and down mines, they cleaned toilets, washed clothes and cooked food, Educated slaves worked as teachers, librarians, artists and even doctors! One in four people in the city of Rome was a slave!

At first, having loads of slaves to do all your work for you seemed like a great thing – nobody else had to lift a finger. Instead you could spend all day pottering around the shops, gossiping to your mates about the latest chariot race or how long it would be before someone suffocated the Emperor with his own underpants.

But having so many slaves turned out to be a bad thing for Rome. People got lazy. Some rich Romans relied so much on their slaves that they couldn't even remember how to dress themselves!

More importantly, lots of poor Romans couldn't get work because the slaves did everything! Without a job, people couldn't afford food and had nothing to do all day. The government had to spend lots of money giving out free grub and putting on gladiator fights to keep everyone amused!

Because this was very expensive, the Emperors kept raising taxes – which made everyone even poorer and very fed up.

RAMPAGING BARBARIANS

As if that wasn't enough to worry about, the Romans also had to deal with hordes of barbarians on the rampage!

Peewee's Notes on How to Spot a Barbarian

The Huns – a fierce bunch of armoured horsemen all the way from Mongolia (near China), led by the legendary 'Attila the Hun'. They rode across Europe, raiding towns, burning and plundering pretty much everything in their path. Everyone was terrified of them: it was said that they drank the blood of their captives and tied the severed heads of their enemies to their saddles.

If you treat us like dogs, we'll bite!

The Goths – (not the kind you see in the city centre today who wear black clothes, big boots and dark eyeliner). These were tribes living on the northern borders of the Roman Empire, who moved to Rome to get away from the horrible Huns. Unfortunately, the Romans weren't very welcoming (refusing to give them any land and only giving them dog meat to eat!). So the Goths got stroppy and took a load of land for themselves.

The Vandals – The Vandals were another tribe who moved into the Empire to escape the Huns. They set up home in North Africa and used ships to sail across the Mediterranean and launch attacks on Roman coastal towns. When the Romans tried to stop them, the Vandals won a sea battle by setting fire to some ships and sailing them into the Roman fleet!

We vandalized those Romans.

The Anglo-Saxons – The Roman army left Britain in 410 AD because Rome needed all its soldiers back home to fight the barbarians. This left the door wide open for the Anglo-Saxons – a group of tribes from across the North Sea. They took over, and it's from them that we get the name 'England' (Angle-land).

These tribes and others like them all moved into the Empire and started setting up their own little kingdoms. There wasn't much the Romans could do about it – their army was big but it wasn't that big: it couldn't fight them all!

Not even the city of Rome was safe – in 410 AD it was invaded by an army of Goths . . . **the first time in 800 years that the city had been attacked!** Thousands of Roman citizens fled to the countryside and many of its grand buildings were trashed.

There are thousands of Roman ruins all over Europe. This is Palmyra in Syria.

ROME? NEVER HEARD OF IT

Eventually, half the Roman Empire collapsed.

The tribes who took over in the West didn't want to speak Latin or wear togas – they had their own languages and their own way of doing things.

Villas, aqueducts and roads fell into ruin, libraries were destroyed and lots of people forgot how to read and write. The Fall of Rome was so traumatic that the centuries after it happened are sometimes called the 'Dark Ages' because of how much was lost.

WE'RE STILL HERE!

But it wasn't all doom and gloom. For a start, the Roman Empire in the East survived!

The capital of the Eastern Empire was Constantinople (now Istanbul in Turkey) and was named after the Emperor who built it – the Emperor **Constantine**.

LOOKING CROSS

In 312 AD, Constantine was about to go into battle when he looked at the sun and saw a cross of light and the words '**If you use this sign, you'll be a winner!**' So he ordered his troops to paint crosses on their shields, and sure enough he won the battle.

Constantine was in York (Eboracum) when he was proclaimed Emperor. His statue is outside York Cathedral.

NO MORE HUMAN SNACKS

Emperor Constantine isn't just famous for building a big city in Turkey. He was also the first Christian Roman Emperor.

The last time I mentioned the Christians they were being fed to lions. But how things change . . .

Understandably, Constantine became a big fan of Christianity. He stopped the persecution of Christians (no more being thrown to lions – hurrah!) and built lots of shiny new churches everywhere.

Constantine even put Jesus on the coins.

By the end of the fourth century, Christianity was the official religion of the Roman Empire and if you worshipped the old gods you were in big trouble (just like the Christians used to be!).

Constantinople became the 'new Rome'. Huge columns, great chunks of marble and beautiful statues were carted across the Empire and used to build the city.

And just in case any nasty barbarians were lurking nearby, the Romans put up enormous walls round it to protect it from attack.

Constantinople became the centre of the Eastern Empire. It was full of palaces, public baths, Roman ideas and Roman inventions – and it lasted another thousand years. **Romulus's dream was still alive.**

Istanbul today is still full of Roman buildings.

Me too!

ROMANS TIMELINE

3000 BC Early hieroglyphs are invented

753 BC Rome starts off as a farming village

509 BC Rome becomes a republic

221– In China, the First Emperor of the Qin
210 BC Dynasty is building up his own empire

216 BC Hannibal thrashes the Romans at the
Battle of Cannae

200 BC The Romans first use concrete

79 BC Pompeii is destroyed when Mount
Vesuvius erupts

73 BC Spartacus breaks out of gladiator
school to lead a slave rebellion

52 BC The Gauls are beaten inside AND out
at the Siege of Alesia

44 BC Julius Caesar is assassinated

27 BC	Rome becomes an Empire, and Octavian is the first person to get the job of Roman Emperor
30 AD	Jesus Christ is crucified by the Romans
37–41 AD	Caligula is Roman Emperor
43 AD	The Romans invade Britain
54–68 AD	Emperor 'Show-Off' Nero is in charge
61 AD	Boudicca clashes with the Romans at the Battle of Watling Street
177–192 AD	Emperor Commodus rules (and kills plenty of lions)
284 AD	Emperor Diocletian chops the Empire into two bits, West and East
312 AD	Emperor Constantine 'sees the light' and becomes a Christian
410 AD	The Roman army gets out of Britain
410 AD	An army of Goths attacks Rome
406–453 AD	Life of Attila the Hun

ROMANS QUIZ

1 Which Carthaginian crazy trekked over the Alps to attack Rome?

2 What did the Romans build to take water from one place to another?

3 What was the Roman version of loo roll?

4 Where's a great place for a business meeting with an ancient Roman?

5 How long did Roman soldiers sign up for?

6 What did Roman schoolkids use instead of paper?

7 What was the Romans' favourite stinky fish sauce called?

8 What did Roman soldiers shout as they formed a tortoise shape?

9 Which sacred bird should you look after if you want to win a battle?

10 Which colour of clothes was illegal for anyone but the Emperor to wear?

Sir Tony Robinson's Weird World of Wonders is a multi-platform extravaganza (which doesn't mean it's a circus in a large railway station). You can get my World of Wonders game on line, there's a website, ebook, audio versions, extra stories and bits of weirdly wonderful design, marketing and publicity. In order to get all those things sorted out, I've surrounded myself with a grown-up version of the Curiosity Crew. They are Gaby Morgan and Fliss Stevens (Editorial), Dan Newman and Tracey Ridgewell (Design), Amy Lines (Marketing), Sally Oliphant (Publicity), James Luscombe (Digital), Tom Skipp (Ebooks) and Becky Lloyd (Audio). A big thanks to them all; they are committed, funny and extremely cool.

Tony has to say that otherwise they'd stop work and go home!

Also available in this series

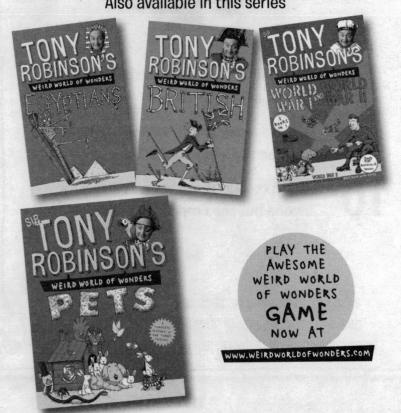